WEALTH WAVES

NAVIGATING THE EBB AND FLOW OF MARKETS

RIK SAYLOR, IAR, CEPA

Rik Saylor-- 1st ed.

ISBN: 978-1-954757-72-1

Author Disclosures:

Any projections, forecasts, probability-of-success scores, Monte Carlo results, or hypothetical illustrations referenced in this book are the output of financial planning software or analytical models. They are based on assumptions—including, but not limited to, assumed rates of return, inflation, spending, tax rates, and life expectancy—that may not occur, and small changes in those assumptions can produce materially different results. These outputs are not guarantees or predictions of future performance, do not reflect the deduction of advisory fees, product expenses, trading costs, or taxes, and are not personalized investment advice. Scores are a point-in-time snapshot and will change as markets, laws, and individual circumstances change.

References to historical events, trends, market cycles, demographic overlays, or specific index or asset-class returns (including the S&P 500) are provided for illustration and educational purposes only. Past performance is not indicative of future results. Market indexes are unmanaged, do not reflect fees or expenses, and cannot be invested in directly. Hindsight descriptions of prior cycles may not reflect the information or uncertainty available in real time, and the author's firm makes no claim of having forecasted any specific market top, bottom, or event. Individual investor results will differ based on timing, costs, taxes, and personal circumstances.

Insurance and annuity products, as well as risk-management strategies, involve costs (including premiums, mortality and expense charges, rider costs, and surrender charges), limitations, exclusions, and conditions that vary by product, carrier, and jurisdiction. Any guarantees associated with an insurance or annuity product are backed solely by the claims-paying ability and financial strength of the issuing insurance company and are not FDIC insured or bank guaranteed. Insurance and annuity products are not suitable for every person or situation, may have tax consequences if modified or surrendered, and should be evaluated against an individual's objectives, time horizon, liquidity needs, and risk tolerance. Readers should review product prospectuses or disclosure documents and consult a licensed insurance professional before purchasing, exchanging, or surrendering any insurance or annuity product.

I would like to dedicate this book to my parents, Jim and Ann Saylor, who showed and modeled the path for me to follow to a successful life—and toward what truly matters.

To my loving and supportive wife, who challenges me every day to be my very best. Her insight and empathy make me a better man.

To my late brother, Jerrl, who unintentionally left me the "gift" of probate. After spending my entire career helping families plan to avoid this maze, I learned difficult but invaluable lessons. I am now more determined than ever to do everything in my power to help others avoid the chaos, confusion, and potential conflict that result from derelict estates.

Last, and most importantly, to my Creator and Savior, Jesus, who has instilled in me a hunger for knowledge and bestowed upon me the gifts and passion to better the lives of those around me.

"By decoding historical and behavioral cycles, Rik delivers a disciplined path to financial independence that cuts through market confusion. It distills the entire process into a four-pillar framework: execute a precise plan, maximize tax-wise growth, protect your wealth from major threats, and secure a lasting legacy."

- Rick Krebs, M&A CPA, CEPA, and author of the books: "Sell Your Business by Design, Not By Default: A Guide to Selling Your Business for More Money" and "Exit Smart"

*"In **Wealth Waves, Navigating the Ebb and Flow of Markets**, Rik Saylor looks at the cyclical nature of equity markets in a way that makes sense to a non-financial person. He then takes practical anecdotes from his own experience and encourages the reader to apply them to planning their own action items. Rik discusses the impact an investor can realize from advance planning for taxes, understanding how risk affects pricing, and the appropriate uses of insurance. **Wealth Waves** is an excellent addition to any financial planning library."*

- John F. Dini, CBEC, CExP, CEPA
  Founder and CEO, ExitMap LLC
  Author of four books: *11 Things You Absolutely Need to Know about Selling Your Business* (2012), and the award-winners *Hunting in a Farmer's World* (2015) and *Your Exit Map* (2017). His latest book for advisors, *The Exit Planning Coach Handbook*, was published in 2022.

These endorsements were given by individuals who are not a current or former client of Rik Saylor Financial and who are not affiliated with the firm. No cash or non-cash compensation was paid or promised in exchange for this endorsement, and the endorsers have no other material conflict of interest in providing it. The endorser's views reflect their own experience and opinions as of the date provided, may not be representative of the experience of clients of the firm, and are not a guarantee of any particular outcome.

Access the Book Resources

Download all companion resources at:

WealthWaveTools.com

Contents

Foreword

When we met, and I interviewed in 2007 for the paraplanner position, some of Rik's first words were, "Where the heck have you been?" He had been searching for over two and a half years, and from that first conversation, I sensed this opportunity was different. I had recently graduated from the University of Cincinnati and begun my career with a large firm, only to feel disillusioned when I was handed a phone book and told to start dialing. I wanted purpose, mentorship, and a place to grow—not just a script.

What I found in Rik was far more than a mentor. Over the past 18 years, he has been a big brother figure, a trusted friend, and, ultimately, a partner as I became an owner of our firm. His belief in people and his willingness to invest in them are two of the defining characteristics of his leadership.

I was immediately impressed by Rik's history. From delivering newspapers at age thirteen to earning Carrier of the Year at fifteen, to becoming a business owner in the construction industry by twenty, his entrepreneurial spirit was evident early on. Those experiences shaped a leader who understands hard work, accountability, and resilience from the ground up.

Rik Saylor, IAR, CEPA

Rik is a visionary leader and innovator in the financial services industry, with over forty-three years of experience. He is a deep thinker—generous, persistent, intelligent, and intuitive—yet always unpretentious and never flashy. He is an avid reader and lifelong student of the markets and history, a critical thinker and healthy skeptic. He says what he means and means what he says. He is also unapologetically intolerant of inefficiency, a trait that drives excellence throughout our organization.

Rik has always said, "We are on a mission—but we're not missionaries."

That mission includes transparent wealth management through Straight Talk – Clear Decisions, a previous educational radio show, the CORE 4 Solutions program, and a truly end-to-end financial services provider. It also includes the Referral Concierge Program, a detailed referral system designed to help people live their ideal lives by connecting them with trusted professionals—from physicians to mechanics and everything in between. We continually ask our clients who they know that provides great service, at a fair price, delivered fairly quickly.

A stickler for detail and excellence, Rik pursued advanced training in business succession planning, earning the CEPA designation in 2020 during the height of COVID. We completed our own succession plan nearly three years ago, reinforcing the long-term vision he has always championed.

Today, Rik continues to lead, manage, and create accountability within our firm and beyond. Through Redde-Zone Business Consulting, a company he founded in April of 2023, he now helps other small business owners do the same—build stronger businesses, better outcomes, and lasting legacies.

I consider myself more of a podcast follower than a reader, yet I thoroughly enjoyed Rik's book. His passion and storytelling truly shine through. I hope and pray that this book benefits you all, helping you live your ideal lives and fulfill your purpose each and every day.

– Eric Hamberg, CFP®

This endorsement was given by Eric Hamberg who is a [partner / officer / employee / owner] of Rik Saylor Financial. As an affiliated person of the firm, Eric receives compensation from the firm in the form of [salary, wages, ownership distributions, profit participation, commissions, or other compensation as applicable]. This affiliation and compensation arrangement constitutes a material conflict of interest because Eric has a direct financial incentive to make favorable statements about the firm. This endorsement reflects Eric's personal opinions, may not be representative of the experience of clients of the firm, is not a guarantee of any particular outcome, and past performance is not indicative of future results.

Introduction

"Knowledge is power."

– Francis Bacon, 1597

If you're reading this, congratulations. In a time when scrolling and soundbites dominate, choosing to read a book is both rare and powerful. As the saying goes, **leaders are readers.**

Let me begin with a simple question:

Why are you reading this book?

What do you hope to gain?

Starting with the end in mind is a guiding principle I've long believed in. When your aim is clear, your chances of hitting the mark—and even surpassing it—increase dramatically.

Let's address the obvious: there is no crystal ball. No perfect tool exists to tell us exactly what will happen, when it will happen, or how. Still, history tends to repeat itself—or at least, as Mark Twain put it: *"It often rhymes."*

Over the past 43+ years in the financial services industry, I've committed my life to understanding and applying the *knowns*—the measurable, repeatable truths that form the foundation of sound financial decision-making. Because let's face it: we don't know what we don't know. That's why seeking out reliable information and verifiable expertise is crucial for shortening your learning curve and helping you hit your goals—on time and on target.

A Consultant's Story

There was a situation at a nuclear plant. Lights were flashing, alarms were blaring, and the employees couldn't figure out what was wrong. The manager contacted a consultant and explained the urgency. "We're willing to pay anything," he said. "Just come and fix this."

The consultant arrived, calmly observed the scene, and took a few moments to assess the situation. Then he walked over to a control panel, flipped a single switch, and instantly everything returned to normal.

Relieved, the staff thanked him profusely. The manager then asked, "What do we owe you?" The consultant replied, "That will be $10,000."

The manager was stunned. "That's outrageous! We're not paying that. How can you justify charging $10,000 just to walk in here and flip a switch?"

The consultant smiled and said, "Traveling here, assessing your situation, and flipping the switch—that was free. Knowing which switch to flip—that's what cost $10,000."

Strategy and Execution

Financial planning and wealth management ultimately come down to two pillars:

1. **Defining a specific strategy, and**
2. **Executing it with discipline and consistency.**

Investing without a game plan is merely hoping things work out well. While I love hope, it's not a good strategy. Like taking a trip without a roadmap, your journey to financial independence without a comprehensive financial plan could negatively affect your outcome. On the other hand, having one is akin to a financial GPS that can dynamically measure and reveal pitfalls that need realignment and adjustment.

Anything less is just noise—and much of that noise comes from the media. I call it *investment pornography*: flashy, emotionally charged, visually stimulating—and mostly useless.

In my experience, many of the talking heads you see on TV are influenced by conflicts of interest. When their predictions are back-tested, few outperform the market—or even match it. To illustrate: more than **90% of professional money managers fail to beat their benchmark index** in a given year. Individual investors tend to do even worse. And those few who do outperform rarely repeat it the following year. Even hedge fund managers—some of the most mathematically driven, data-focused traders in the world—win on just **55% to 65%** of their trades. That's better than the local weather forecast, but it's still only slightly better than a coin toss.

The takeaway? Focus on what's measurable. Most people will not outsmart hedge funds or beat the market with day trading. During the 1990s, when day trading was at its peak, research showed that **90% of day traders lost 100% of their capital.**

Similarly, at the casinos near where I live in southwest Ohio, **89% of gamblers walk away with nothing.** Those beautiful buildings weren't funded by winners—and neither was Las Vegas.

Pulling Back the Curtain on Oz

This book is designed to **demystify** and **simplify** an industry that, in my opinion, is second only to nuclear energy in terms of complexity and regulation—and only about half as dangerous. My goal is to take you behind the curtain, revealing what top financial professionals **know**, **do**, and **avoid**—so that you can apply those insights to your own financial life.

We'll focus on **four key areas** that form the foundation of lasting financial success:

1. Strategic Planning with Precision Tools

Begin by crafting a personalized strategy—tailored to your goals, risk tolerance, and timeline. Then utilize modern tools and technology to model and stress-test that strategy under different market conditions. While no plan can guarantee outcomes, probability-based planning tools are designed to help illustrate a range of possible results under stated assumptions. Any projection depends on the inputs, the assumptions used, and the market scenarios modeled, and actual results will differ. Ongoing monitoring, discipline, and adjustments as circumstances change are part of the planning process generally.

> *Any projections, forecasts, probability-of-success scores, Monte Carlo results, or hypothetical illustrations referenced in this book are the output of financial planning software or analytical models. They are based on assumptions—including, but not limited to, assumed rates of return, inflation, spending, tax rates, and life expectancy—that may not occur, and small changes in those assumptions can produce materially different results. These outputs are not guarantees or predictions of future performance, do not reflect the deduction of advisory fees, product expenses, trading costs, or taxes, and are not personalized investment advice. Scores are a point-in-time snapshot and will change as markets, laws, and individual circumstances change.*

2. Tax Efficiency

Borrowing from the words of Jesus: *"What does it profit a man to gain the whole world, yet forfeit his soul?"* (Mark 8:36)

In the financial world, a similar question could be asked:

"What does it profit an investor to build significant wealth, only to lose much of it to taxes?"

Depending on your state of residence, the primary financial threats include **income tax**, **capital gains tax**, **probate costs**, and **estate tax**.

As of 2025, and with the enactment of the OneBigBeautifulBill (OBBB):

Estate & Gift Tax Exemption

- Per-individual exemption raised to **$15 million** (from ~$13.99M in 2025), effective Jan 1, 2026

- Married couples exempt up to **$30 million** jointly
- Indexed for inflation annually starting in 2026, with 2025 as the base year

To win this game, you must first **identify your opponents** and then implement proven, legal strategies designed to reduce the erosion of your wealth and preserve what you've built for future generations.

3. Risk Management and Protection

You've spent a lifetime building what you have—so it only makes sense to protect it. We'll explore how to evaluate risks, decide whether to **retain**, **transfer**, or **manage** them, and understand the financial tools available for doing so. Risk management isn't about fear—it's about intelligent decision-making.

4. Legacy and Estate Planning

This subject is deeply personal for me. About two years ago, I lost the last of my immediate family—my closest brother. Despite my decades of industry experience, his estate turned out to be the most difficult I've ever dealt with. He hadn't named me as executor or trustee, which meant I had to be appointed administrator by the court. While I had long understood estate planning academically, this experience made it painfully real.

When done properly, legacy planning can ensure a **smooth and meaningful transition**. When neglected, it often leads to **confusion**, **unnecessary costs**, **possible conflict**, and **lost opportunities**. We'll explore the **good**, the **bad**, and the **preventable** aspects of this crucial area. Focusing your legacy on the "WHY" you are choosing the planning you will do, rather than merely the number of years you were here on earth or between the "dashes," could be the difference between good and great.

Whether you're reading this on a screen or holding a printed copy—as I personally prefer—I encourage you to **highlight key passages**, **take notes**, **dog-ear pages, perform the Identify-Plan-Action (IPA) exercises** that resonate with you, and take the first step! Financial planning can sometimes feel like a merry-go-round, but the **fundamentals don't change**.

To get the most out of this book, adopt the Greek idea of praxis.

Think of knowledge as theory, and action as the steps you take. But praxis is where the real work happens—it's the moment you begin adjusting, refining, and evolving those steps in real time, guided by the results you experience.

This book is not just meant to be read. It is meant to be lived, tested, and reshaped through your own actions.

So sit back. Take a deep breath. And prepare to learn what the **smartest investors already know**.

This is your invitation to take control of your financial future—with **clarity**, **confidence**, and **purpose**.

– *Rik Saylor*

1 History, Demographics, and Cyclical Analysis

"History repeats itself, and if it doesn't, it sure rhymes a lot."

— Samuel Clemens (Mark Twain)

From an early age, I have been fascinated by human behavior—*psychology*, the study of individual actions, and *sociology*, the study of how the masses behave. History serves as the scorecard of these collective decisions. Behavioral finance, in essence, is history applied to money. I have observed that there appear to be *"opportunities and perils in every market."*

Understanding *who* behaves a certain way, *why* they do so, and *when* they are likely to act is both fascinating and, at times, profitable.

Cause and effect in human behavior is as much art as it is science—and marketing has long thrived on this principle. It's a macro (trend/high-level) vs. micro (metrics/numbers) view of the potential causes and effects of where the market has been and may be going.

Today, metadata is collected around the clock to predict and influence our decisions as consumers. It's reminiscent of "Big Brother" from George Orwell's *1984*. For a modern perspective on that idea, the 2018 documentary *The Creepy Line* offers an eye-opening look at how data now drives persuasion.

History consistently reveals that human behavior is cyclical and predictable. We are creatures of habit. Applying this understanding to investing is not only logical—it's essential.

The Demographic Connection

In the early 2000s, I became intrigued by demographic research that compared U.S. birth rates (adjusted for immigration) with movements in the Dow Jones Industrial Average. When these charts were overlaid, patterns emerged that appeared to forecast market trends based on population shifts and spending habits. Analysts who modeled these demographic and economic overlays believed a bubble cycle could develop.

At its core, the idea is simple: *major in the major economic factors.* The largest drivers of the U.S. economy are predictable because they are based on life stage behaviors and technology waves.. Peak spenders in the U.S. are typically between the ages of 46 and 50. Personal Consumption Expenditures (PCE)—the sum of what consumers buy—accounts for roughly two-thirds of U.S. GDP.

The Spending Wave

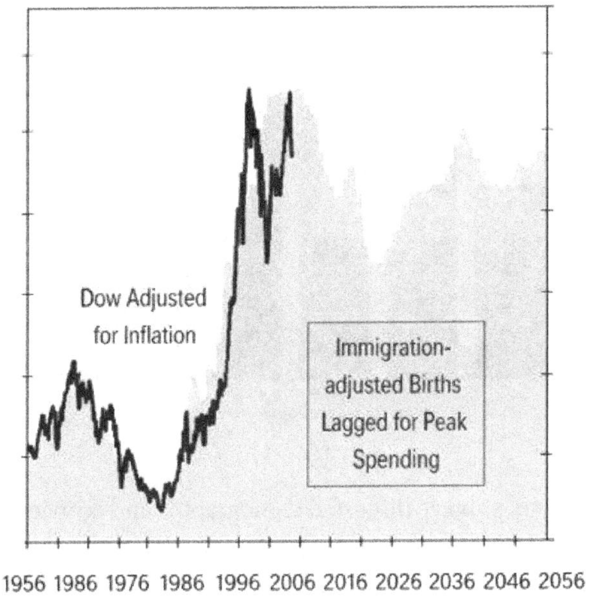

The top two categories in which Americans go into debt are housing and automobiles. The reselling of these same assets ranks close behind. The median U.S. home price now exceeds $400,000, and the average vehicle costs around $48,000. Each purchase fuels a web of jobs and services—construction, sales, financing, and manufacturing.

The Peak Spenders

The 46-to-50-year-old demographic represents established earners at the top of their earnings, often with children in college and at peak financial responsibilities. The more individuals in this age group, the stronger the overall economic demand—and, by extension, the greater the momentum markets tend to have.

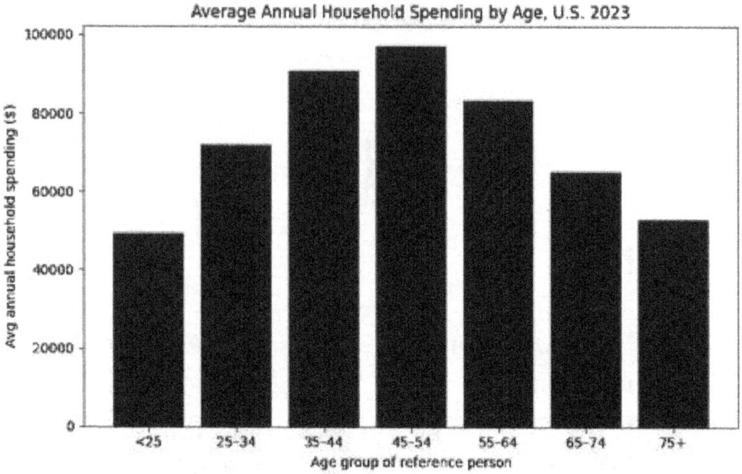

Some analysts publicly discussed demographic and economic overlays and suggested parallels to prior cycles such as the late 1920s. These views were one perspective among many at the time and, like all market forecasts, could not be verified in advance. Past market cycles and demographic trends are shown here for educational context only and do not predict future results. After all, housing and the stock market were booming through the late 1990s and early 2000s. Home sizes and prices were exploding, luxury cars filled driveways, and easy credit made it all seem sustainable. I remember thinking, *"Everybody can't be drug dealers—somebody's got to be buying this stuff!"* It was a humorous way to acknowledge the excess building beneath the surface.

This same demographic group has now entered a peak spending wave of medical care services, which begins around 50 and continues until death. There will need to be significant changes in how we pay for these services to avoid a possible collapse of the system. It would be wise to plan for this, as it is the #2 major concern for pre-retirees and retirees, according to a 2013 Gallup poll.

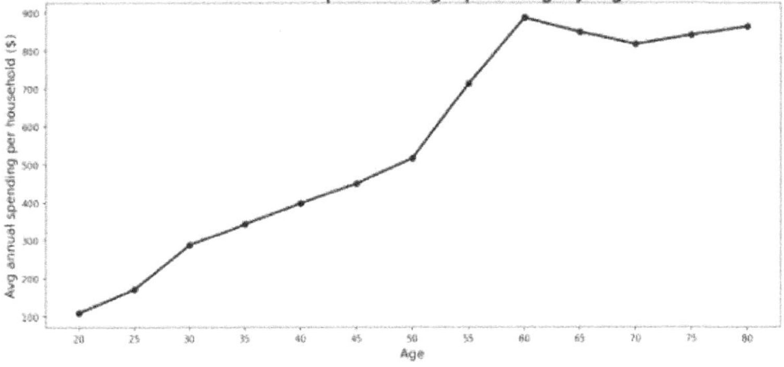

Source: U.S. Bureau of Labor Statistics, Consumer Expenditure Survey (2023)

The Technology Impact

It's interesting to note how we discover or uncover technologies that make life more efficient, productive, and easier in some way. To have a major impact, technology needs to change the way the masses live their everyday lives, be adopted by large numbers of consumers, and put a lot of people to work.

The Grand Supercycle, 1700–2010

The first boom/bust bubble on the chart above represents the steam engine and the beginning of the Industrial Revolution. The second one begins around 1830-1837, caused by the Transportation Revolution, and has a second boom/bust effect from 1848-1857. There was a stock market crash and a mini-depression that followed in 1873-1879, driven by overexpansion, speculation, and monetary tightening (see TV series "Hell on Wheels").

The automobile was the next innovation in transportation beginning around 1910-1930s. From the manufacturing of Ford's Model T, assembly line production and higher wages around 1913, mass-market auto financing around 1915-1919, to mass consumer adoption and saturation in the late 1920s, eventually leading to the stock market crash of 1929.

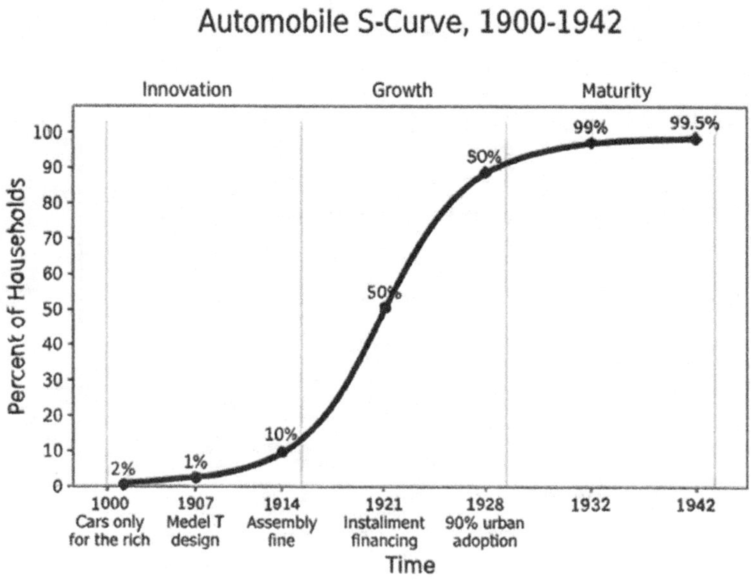

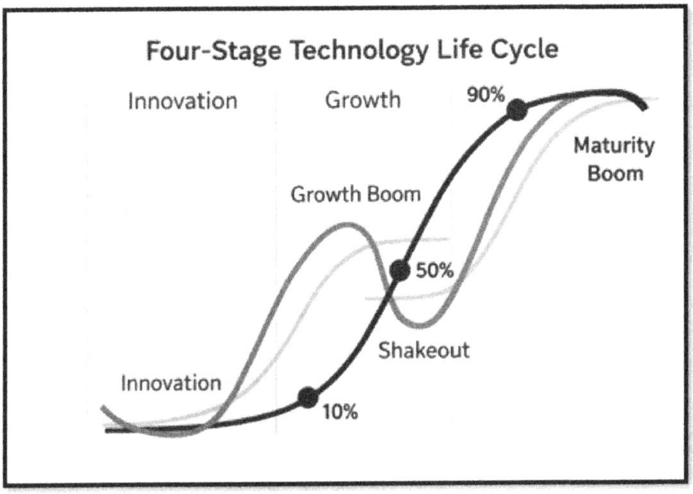

A seemingly common pattern appears for most, if not all, new major technologies and inventions. In the beginning, there is a crowd of producers. Second, there is a "shakeout" and consolidation that occur as the strong buy out the smaller, less viable ones. Lastly, the survivors become thrivers and continue until critical mass and adoption are achieved.

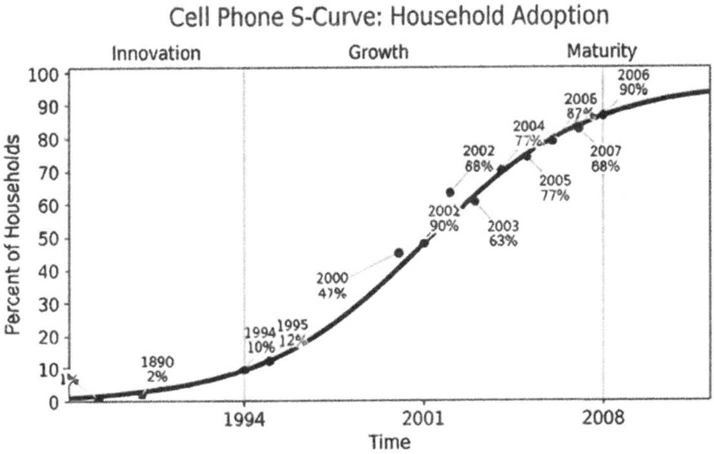

The information and telecommunications computing wave began around the mid- to late 1970s and included cellular phones and high-speed broadband technologies, culminating in a peak in mid 2008.

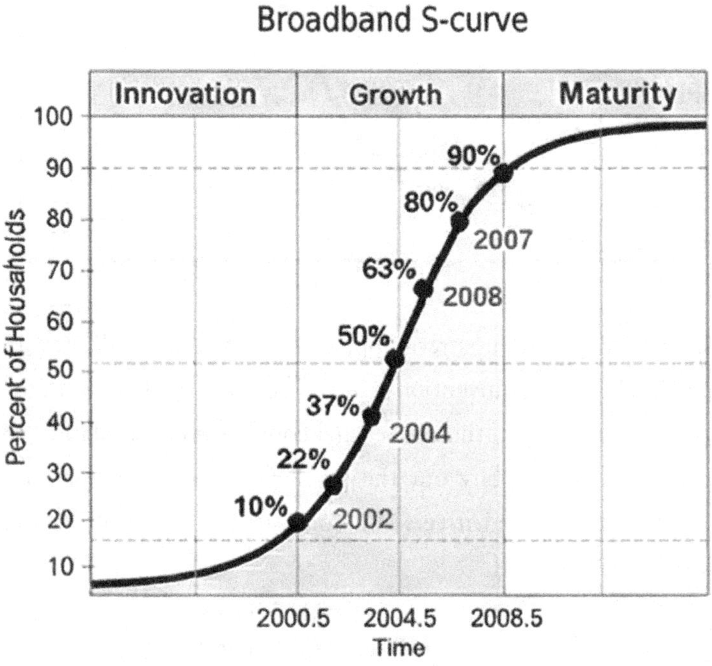

Note that these 3 major technologies were coming into their own on a common timeline that coincided with the Baby Boom Generation reaching their peak spending ages of 46-50. This appears to be the largest number (peaking around 79 million in 1999-2001) to migrate through the peak spending cycle in the richest country in the history of the world.

The stock market also reached all-time highs, only to crash and enter the Great Recession in October 2008. Cause and effect or mere coincidence? While no crystal ball can predict our future, there certainly appears to be a rhyme and reason here.

All of these cycles mirror the following chart closely:

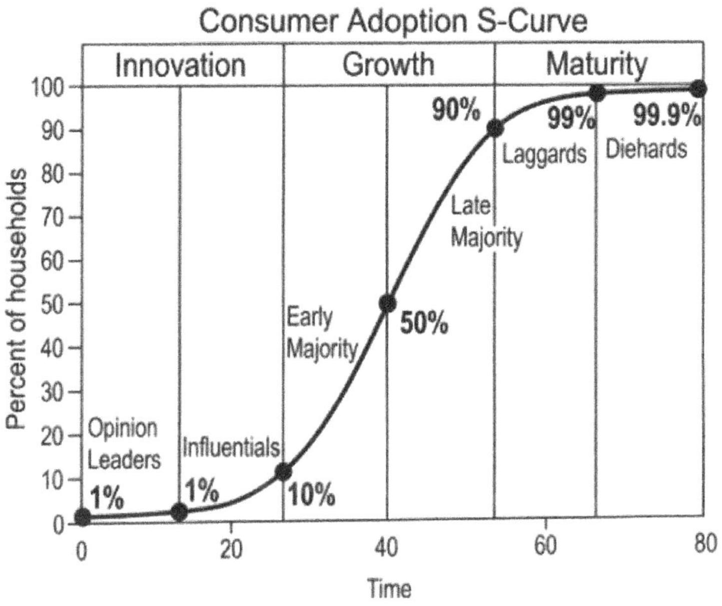

The Housing Bubble

Behind the scenes, a perfect storm was forming. Banks and investors were leveraging the economy to unprecedented levels, fueled by the behavior of the baby boom generation and policy shifts from Washington. Terms like *subprime mortgages, no-doc loans*, and *drive-by appraisals* entered our vocabulary. Banks, once conservative institutions, discarded traditional lending prudence.

This shift began in the late 1990s, when the Clinton administration and Attorney General Janet Reno pressured banks to extend mortgages to low- and moderate-income borrowers. Those who didn't comply risked losing access to the Federal Reserve system—effectively their lifeline. Years later, President Bill Clinton would reflect, "We thought it was a good idea at the time."

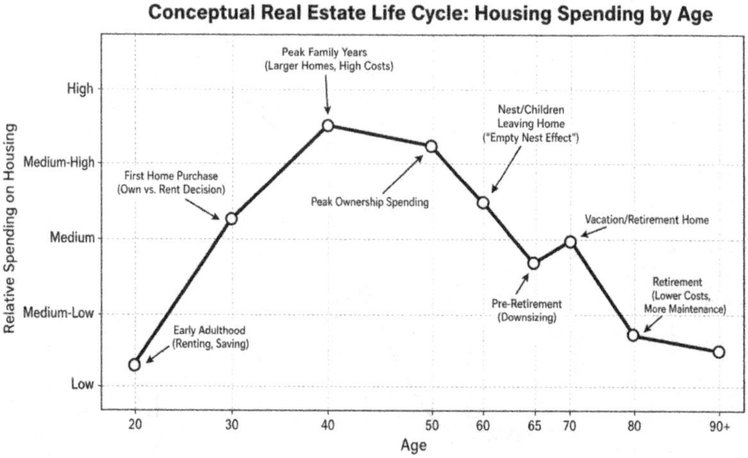

The housing explosion fueled the peak spender baby boom wave and coincided with the major computer/telecommunications wave, like never before in modern history.

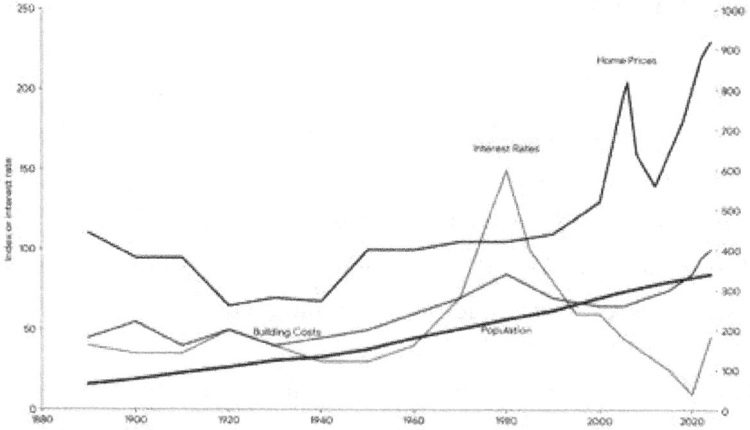

Wall Street amplified the risk. Through securitization, lenders bundled mortgages into complex financial products—Collateralized Mortgage Obligations (CMOs) and Collateralized Debt Obligations (CDOs)—and sold them worldwide. It was like pouring gasoline on a fire. These instruments were marketed as safe investments, yet they were built on shaky foundations.

As depicted in the documentary *House of Cards* and dramatized in *The Big Short*, the web of interconnected investors meant that when the system cracked, it did so globally. Dr. Michael Burry, played by Christian Bale in *The Big Short*, recognized the fragility early and bet against the market. In one memorable scene, he visits Goldman Sachs and observes young traders confidently declaring, "Mortgages never fail." Ironically, while firms like Goldman were selling long positions to bullish investors, they were simultaneously selling short positions to others—betting on both sides of the trade.

When the crash came, it was the largest financial collapse since the Great Depression. And in a darkly comic twist, Burry—one of the few who saw it coming—was rewarded not with gratitude but with several IRS audits.

> *References to historical events, trends, market cycles, demographic overlays, or specific index or asset-class returns (including the S&P 500) are provided for illustration and educational purposes only. Past performance is not indicative of future results. Market indexes are unmanaged, do not reflect fees or expenses, and cannot be invested in directly. Hindsight descriptions of prior cycles may not reflect the information or uncertainty available in real time, and the author's firm makes no claim of having forecasted any specific market top, bottom, or event. Individual investor results will differ based on timing, costs, taxes, and personal circumstances.*

How Risk-Management Principles Can Be Applied During a Downturn

Leading up to 2008, various commentators discussed demographic and housing-cycle indicators. Some of those discussions ultimately aligned with what later occurred, but this alignment is only visible in hindsight and does not mean similar forecasts can be relied on in the future. Markets, housing cycles, and economic conditions are influenced by many factors, and past patterns are discussed here solely for educational context. Housing began a precipitous fall. Banks doubled and tripled down in their attempt to keep the party going, to no avail. They were widely viewed as "too big to fail" by many running the systems in place.

The timing of the eventual correction could not be predicted. Based on the signals being publicly discussed at the time, we reviewed client allocations and, where appropriate and consistent with each client's objectives, recommended adjustments intended to reduce equity exposure. Individual results varied based on each client's situation, timing, and the positions they held, and this narrative is illustrative of the process rather than representative of any particular client's outcome. We would regularly ask our clients the market math question: "if you lose 50% how much will it take to get back to even? Answer: 100%! Don't lose 50%!

Markets and housing both experienced precipitous corrections initially around -50%. The S&P 500 settled out at roughly -37% losses.

Not Everyone Heeded Our Advice

We held public speaking events during this prelude to the collapse and attracted a large number of clients who followed our guidance. One couple, in particular, had come from these events and initially listened and followed our recommendations.

They were elder stage, west siders in Cincinnati, and they had done quite well as residential home builders during the housing boom and had grown accustomed to a lifestyle that matched. They had experienced the market shakeout in the early 2000s and had taken considerable losses while represented by a well-known local bank investment department. We were hired around the middle of 2006 by this couple with investable assets of around $700,000, after their peak of $2 million had come and gone.

The bank investment representative told them that their income draw was sustainable even after the tremendous loss they had sustained, and to "stay the course because it will come back." Quite to the contrary, I explained to them that they were experiencing "reverse dollar cost averaging" by continuing to draw down at the rate they were receiving, rather than the prudent rate of withdrawal, which closely matches the RMD (Required Minimum Distributions) life expectancy tables for IRA-type accounts. Furthermore, the damage they inflicted compounded the damage to their investments and was most likely irreparable. RULE: All spending damages wealth! To minimize it, take from the "winners" vs. the down positions.

I was fond of them, as they were us, as the struggle to correct the course continued. Some clients require a more counseling approach, and these folks were the epitome of that. Most of our meetings focused on budget discussions and conflict over who was spending the most money and what it was being spent on. Meeting after meeting, this couple would have me referee their budget battle as I recommended the most basic principle of all: spend less than your inflows, or you will end up living with your children!

Eventually, after a year and a half of back-and-forth in mid 2008, we met with their 3 grown children in an effort to help them. Unfortunately, a couple of months post "intervention," they met with me to inform me that they were moving their accounts away from us. My parting words were that I foresee a 50% downturn and that we should at least hold our products and positions until the storm passes. His parting words… "I don't think that is going to happen." Of course, in October 2008, the market sold off 50% and came back eventually to net a loss of -37%. I didn't receive a thank-you call …

Patterns in Behavior and History

The cycles of individual behavior (psychology) and mass behavior (sociology) ultimately shape what we call history. Few works capture these generational dynamics better than *The Fourth Turning* (1997) by William Strauss and Neil Howe. I personally consider this one of the most profound books I've ever read and referenced.

The Four Turnings

A *turning* is a shift in social mood that occurs as generational archetypes move into new phases of life. Each lasts roughly a generation—about 20 to 25 years.

- **The First Turning – The High (Spring)**
  A confident, unified era marked by strong institutions and low individualism. Society is stable and optimistic. Outward focus as institutions are stronger, individualism is weaker.
- **The Second Turning – The Awakening (Summer)**
  A passionate period of spiritual and cultural renewal. The established order is challenged by emerging new values. Inward focus as individualism/spirituality pushes back on institutions/protocols as necessary.
- **The Third Turning – The Unraveling (Fall)**
  Results from individualism rising, institutions weakening, and social cohesion fraying. People pursue personal freedom over collective purpose. Income/wealth disparity widens.
- **The Fourth Turning – The Crisis (Winter)**
  A time of upheaval when the old system collapses, and a new civic order emerges. It is both destructive and regenerative—a rebirth through challenge and the "fire."

The Generational Archetypes

Generations repeat in a recurring pattern of four archetypes:

- **Prophets** are born during a High, come of age during an Awakening, lead during an Unraveling, and grow old in a Crisis.
- **Nomads** are born during an Awakening, come of age during an Unraveling, and mature during a Crisis.
- **Heroes** are born during an Unraveling, come of age in a Crisis, and dominate in a High.
- **Artists** are born during a Crisis, come of age in a High, and bring empathy during the next Awakening.

Generations are defined by 3 factors: a common location in history, common beliefs/behaviors, and a perceived "membership" in the group. Because of these, a generation develops a collective persona (archetype).

Why Does This Matter?

At any given time, these archetypes interact to shape the cultural and economic tides of history. The rhythm of these cycles—roughly every 80 to 100 years—**reveals not only how societies evolve but how economies rise, peak, and reset.** As archetypes migrate through the repeating cycles of time, their behaviors are fairly predictable, their respective choices impacting the current period and writing the future. The pattern repeats in large part because the generations born at the beginning of the cycle are passing away before the start of the next one.

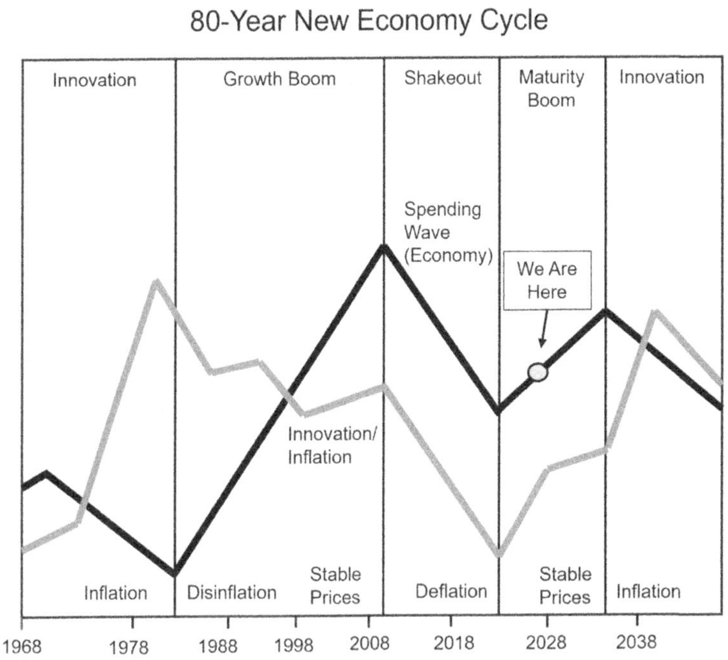

Artificial Intelligence — Opportunities and Perils

AI (Artificial Intelligence) is a phenomenon that almost seems like science fiction. It has the potential to profoundly change the way we live, receive medical treatment, are governed, and interact, work, play, and are entertained.

For those who say they aren't interested and will "opt out" of this wave, it may already be too late. A recent Gallup Poll (1/15/2025) suggested that a large majority of Americans already use AI in some form, even though many don't realize it. If you own and use a cell phone, use Google search, or a multitude of apps, you're already participating. From weather apps to Amazon, movie streaming services to social media platforms, artificial intelligence is increasingly embedded in the digital products we use daily.

For example, John Deere's AI-powered herbicide sprayer uses cameras and machine learning to spray only weeds, potentially reducing farmers' chemical costs and improving food quality, according to Ben Sherry, "Even John Deere Is Getting in on the AI Boom." (3/26/2024).

In March 2024, University of Kentucky Students harnessed AI to decode passages from an ancient scroll scorched by Mt. Vesuvius's AD 79 eruption.

From the East Coast's Massachusetts, throughout the Midwest, to the West Coast's California, states are deploying AI to help ease traffic bottlenecks and analyze sewer systems, potentially saving taxpayers time and money, according to Mark Jackley, "Using AI in Local Government: 10 Use Cases" (8/7/2024).

Recently, so-called "smart glasses" with built-in facial recognition have demonstrated the ability to quickly identify individuals and surface publicly available data as they pass by.

Images from Arnold Schwarzenegger's movie "Terminator" flash the potential perils and darker possibilities that may exist within this technology as well.

AI is rapidly becoming ubiquitous and may soon form part of the foundational "rails" the world runs on. As President Trump's AI Action Plan has stated, the age of AI represents "an Industrial Revolution, an information revolution, and a renaissance all at once."

From my perspective, we are still in the early innings of this evolution, as an enormous amount of capital expenditure and new entrants continue to flood the field. In addition, expectations remain very high for the potential payoff and impact.

To recognize and potentially take advantage of this wave will require focus and expertise as AI progresses from its early stages, through a potential shakeout and consolidation, into broader mass adoption, and ultimately toward maturity. A familiar boom-to-bust cycle may emerge once again.

Despite its promise, AI also carries meaningful risks. Capital is flowing aggressively into the space, often ahead of fully proven returns, raising the possibility of overinvestment and valuation bubbles. Regulatory scrutiny is increasing, and rapid innovation could compress margins as competition intensifies. As with past technological revolutions, not all early leaders will ultimately succeed.

The Evolution of Intelligence

"After thousands of years of compounding scientific discovery and technological progress, we have figured out how to melt sand, add some impurities, arrange it with astonishing precision at extraordinarily tiny scale into computer chips, run energy through it, and end up with systems capable of creating increasingly capable artificial intelligence. This may turn out to be the most consequential fact about all of history so far."

— **Sam Altman,** CEO OpenAI / ChatGPT

The question today of how far and high AI may take us is yet to be seen as it continues to unfold.

This framework isn't perfect, but it is remarkably consistent. The patterns of psychology, political science, sociology, and philosophy, layered over time, can possibly help explain why markets move the way they do—and why history, even when it doesn't repeat, most certainly rhymes. It reminds me of what Wayne Gretzky (the great one in hockey) famously replied when asked how he scored so many goals: "I skate to where the puck is going to be, not where it has been."

Ecclesiastes 3:1–8 King Solomon

To every thing there is a season,
and a time to every purpose under heaven:
a time to be born, and a time to die;
a time to plant, and a time to pluck up that which is planted;
a time to kill, and a time to heal;
a time to break down, and a time to build up;
a time to weep, and a time to laugh;
a time to mourn, and a time to dance;
a time to cast away stones, and a time to gather stones together;
a time to embrace, and a time to refrain from embracing;
a time to get, and a time to lose;
a time to keep, and a time to cast away;
a time to rend, and a time to sew;
a time to keep silent, and a time to speak;
a time to love, and a time to hate;
a time of war, and a time of peace.

KEY TAKEAWAYS

- Human behavior moves in clear, predictable cycles. When you understand who is acting, why they're acting, and where they are in life, market trends begin to make a lot more sense, presenting possible opportunities and pitfalls.
- Demographics, especially the 46–50 peak-spending group, seem to drive the bulk of economic demand, and their transitions through life stages reliably shape the direction of the economy.
- The stock market and housing bubbles were not random; they may have resulted from predictable behavioral excess, demographic pressures, and policy decisions that pushed banks and consumers into unsustainable risk.
- Generational cycles (about 20 years), as outlined in *The Fourth Turning*, reveal how social moods rise, peak, fracture, and reset, providing a framework for understanding long-term market, political, and societal shifts.
- History may not repeat exactly, but its rhythm is unmistakable. Recognizing that rhythm is essential to understanding markets, managing risk, and preparing for the next cycle.
- Fundamentals are a constant: Live on less than you bring in; withdrawals damage wealth, so adhere to the "prudent rate of withdrawal" based on growing/expanding (up) holdings vs. contracting ones (down). Take from up vs. down positions to minimize the damage.

Your IPAs (Not the Beer)

Write your *Identify Plan Actions* here:

IDENTIFIED item(s):

PLAN (your strategy):

ACTIONS (take a step forward):

2

Element One: Strategy Part One

Without a plan, you're just winging it.

When I started my first company in my early twenties—a construction business—I couldn't imagine bidding on a job, let alone completing one, without a blueprint. The blueprint wasn't just a formality; it was a plan that forced me to think through the process, anticipate challenges, and identify efficiencies before the first nail was ever driven. Working through a plan on paper—considering contingencies and optimizing for the ideal outcome—simply made sense. That same principle applies directly to the world of finance.

If the goal is financial independence, then a structured, well-developed plan is essential. Today's technology allows us to use advanced planning tools that factor in income, expenses, investable assets, taxes, inflation, and historical market performance through back-testing. These tools generate projections based on the inputs provided (income, expenses, investable assets, taxes, inflation assumptions, and historical market data used for back-testing). The purpose is to illustrate a range of possible outcomes under stated assumptions, not to predict the future. Results depend entirely on the assumptions used, and actual outcomes will vary.

| *Please see Author Disclosures*

A strategy, however, is not static. It must evolve. Regular reviews and adjustments should reflect real-life changes—unexpected expenses, healthcare needs, support for children or grandchildren, lifestyle changes, or long-held bucket list goals. Paying close attention to the respective phase you are presently in is paramount. Accumulation (building assets), Growth (maximizing values), Preservation (protecting capital), and Distribution (spending assets). There are unique, time-tested characteristics that are fundamentally sound. Know them and adhere to them.

Dividing and distinguishing which money bucket you are building is also very important.

- ➔ **Short-Range:** Liquid savings get the highest possible, safe rate of return. Check credit unions, online banks, and money market funds.
- ➔ **Mid-Range:** Look for a better rate of return (i.e., bank CDs), a little less liquidity, and reasonable safety.
- ➔ **Long-Range:** The "rest of your life" type investments. Traditional/ROTH IRAs, 401(k)s, and employer-sponsored

plans fit this category. It's also a good idea to balance taxable, tax-deferred, and tax-free, because we don't know what tax rates will be!

The Tortoise (Turtle) vs. the Hare (Rabbit) Couple

I developed and taught a curriculum in an adult learning program at two local universities. I encountered many successful adult students over 5 years of teaching, enlightening and motivating them with the principles of financial success.

One particular student, and later client, engaged my firm for wealth management services. He and his wife were very successful business owners in landscaping during the residential/commercial building boom.

While he was the risk-taking, visionary entrepreneur, she was the cautious, integrator-operations person. Together, they made a great team, and their finances and lives matched that.

As we met regularly, she listened and planned, while he speculated and "gambled" in their separate accounts. As fiduciaries, we accommodated them both in style and the positions recommended and executed.

He had accounts held away that he was investing in leveraged options that were 2-3x the base amount invested. When the market rose, he experienced a similar 2-3x unrealized returns. However, on the downside, it had the same effect. Our firm didn't represent him in these positions and held the more balanced portion of his overall portfolio.

Rule: Use risk with a budget! Like a baseball lineup, a couple of home run hitters are enough. While they hit the most home runs, they also have the highest strikeout percentage!

His wife adhered to her risk tolerance and the financial plan we had created for them, and was a patient, "steady as she goes" (tortoise-turtle) type, focused on the end goals. In addition, we had a mini-class-type meeting with their young adult children, including the son who was the successor to the family business.

The differences in style among them were both contrasting and challenging. Like a horse race, you can bet on one horse or "win, place, or show." All or nothing vs. possibly winning something with a smaller payoff. The latter of these two approaches is the epitome of disciplined wealth management. Neither is the right or wrong way to invest; however, I view it as strategic and tactical. Tactical, potential "win" positions are like spices in a recipe; don't overdo it. The other market axiom is: There are bulls, bears, and hogs...hogs get slaughtered!

In the end, the father/husband's approach (hare-rabbit) went from feast to famine, as so many "casino approaches" and "get rich quick/fast" behaviors do. His no-plan, roll-the-dice method worked well during the business-growth phase, but did not translate profitably into his execution phase of wealth management/accumulation.

Travel with a GPS

For most people, the ultimate objective of financial independence is simple: the confidence that they will not run out of money before they run out of life. The most effective modern financial planning platforms integrate live data feeds from all assets and continuously compare actual performance against long-term goals. This creates a dynamic and responsive planning environment.

These state-of-the-art technological wonders, while not a guarantee, can estimate potential outcomes based on inflows vs. outflows, incorporating projected returns and beta (stress) testing across a multitude of market scenarios over past markets/cycles and in addition, measuring erosion of the portfolio from taxes, withdrawals, as well as an individual's goals, bucket list spending, and legacy gifting to heirs. What is produced is a mathematical probability of possible success or failure. Used thoughtfully, these tools can serve as a kind of 'financial navigation system' — not a guarantee, but a way to periodically compare actual progress against long-term goals and adjust as circumstances change. The aim is to support informed decision-making over time; outcomes depend on markets, personal choices, and assumptions that will not all prove accurate.

After 43 years in the financial services industry, I am still surprised by how many people talk about retirement without ever completing a comprehensive financial plan. It's no different than someone arriving at an airport expecting to buy a ticket and board a plane, without knowing the destination, securing accommodations, or even confirming that the place exists! The old adage, *"Begin with the end in mind,"* is not just good advice—it is the foundation of every sound strategic plan.

Please see Author Disclosures

Download the Wealth Waves Gameplan Strategy and all the resources from this book at: *WealthWaveTools.com*

KEY TAKEAWAYS

- A financial plan works the same way a construction blueprint does; it forces you to think ahead, anticipate challenges, and make smarter decisions before taking action. "Measure twice but cut once."
- Modern planning tools allow you to test assumptions, account for taxes, inflation, and real-life variables, and build the most informed path toward financial independence.
- A good strategy must evolve as life changes. Healthcare needs, family support, lifestyle shifts, and unexpected events all require adjustment.
- Three buckets of money serve different roles in your portfolio: short-range, mid-range, and long-range. This is a good comparison tool for short-range savings. Here's a link: ***WealthWaveTools.com.***
- Financial independence ultimately comes down to one core objective: confidence that your money will last as long as you do.
- Beginning with the end in mind is the foundation of a real strategy and the reason a comprehensive plan must come before any meaningful financial decision.

Your IPAs (Not the Beer)

Write your *Identify Plan Actions* here:

IDENTIFIED item(s):

PLAN (your strategy):

ACTIONS (take a step forward):

3

Element One: Execution Part Two

Markets go up, down, and sideways...
strategies should shift for each one.

The market is said to run on supply and demand. When demand rises, and supply tightens, prices go up — simple economics. But markets are rarely that simple.

One of my favorite discoveries is a phenomenon called "priced in." It happens when supply and demand are so far out of balance that the trade seems "too obvious." When that happens, the forces behind the market often *discount* a crowded trade, and the price of the position falls instead of rising. In short, when everyone sees the same easy trade, it stops being easy. Rule: Wall Street doesn't provide slam dunks!

Wall Street lives by an old rhythm — *buy the rumor, sell the news.* That means traders often act on whispers and speculation before an event, taking a position on instinct or on inside knowledge. When the news becomes official, they sell. The profit is made in anticipation, not confirmation.

Market professionals also track what's called **smart money** and **dumb money**. One of the best-known examples is the AAII (American Association of Individual Investors) Sentiment Survey — a contrarian indicator. When the majority of investors are too euphoric (overbought) or too fearful (oversold), market makers often take the opposite side. The crowd is usually late to the party.

"Smart money" refers to institutional investors — hedge funds, pension funds, and the heavy hitters on Wall Street. The bond market is often called the *smarter* market because it tends to recognize turning points in trends before the equity markets do.

Hedge funds, in particular, have built intricate systems to track sentiment and momentum, often spotting the trade before the move even begins. If you've seen the TV series *Billions*, you've watched the character Bobby Axelrod turn this into an art form — harvesting information, manipulating circumstances, and creating pressure to make a specific outcome inevitable. Is it art or science? Probably a little bit of both.

Unless you're an insider on Wall Street — or in Congress, where some lawmakers still trade on pending legislation — you're playing the same game as the rest of us, but without the privileged information. The conflict of interest in that dynamic is staggering. A recent comparison revealed that a particular congresswoman has outperformed Warren Buffett's Berkshire Hathaway fund...maybe she was just really lucky!

Even hedge fund managers — the world's most sophisticated traders — only get it right about 55% to 65% of the time. And it's worth remembering that *more money is often made on the short side* of markets than on the long. Fear moves faster than greed.

Please see Author Disclosures

Download the "Wealth Waves Risk Range Finder" and all the resources from this book at: *WealthWaveTools.com*

The human condition ensures that most investment decisions are driven by **emotion first, logic later.** Behavioral finance has proven this again and again: investors chase headlines, buy near peaks, and sell in despair at the bottom. That's "dumb money" in action — not because people are foolish, but because emotion is powerful and markets are designed to exploit it.

Even professional fund managers aren't immune. Many underperform their benchmarks — the index they're supposed to beat — precisely because emotion sneaks into their strategy. Enhanced Index funds (ETFs-Exchange Traded Funds, SPDRs -Standard and Poor's Depository Receipts), by contrast, have no emotions at all. They don't panic, they don't celebrate, and they never sell too soon or hold too long.

The Human Forecasting Model

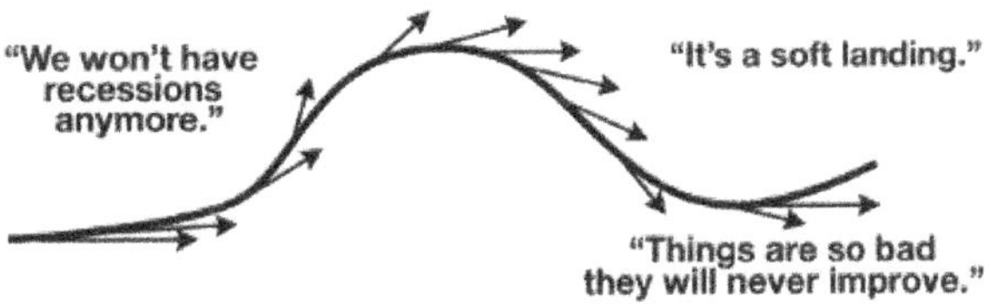

A Story of Missed Opportunities

I was interviewing a potential client in my office around 2011. His story was an interesting example filled with intrigue and lightning strikes. He was a very honorable veteran of the Vietnam War era of the 1960s, in logistics. He and a comrade were associated with the beginning of the Internet (ARPANET). No, it was *not* invented by Al Gore or Bill Gates.

As both of them were nearing the end of their enlistments, his associate suggested that they take their reenlistment signing bonuses and start a side business related to the soon-to-be arena of personal computers. He passed on this and chose instead to save the money for a home purchase or some other goals. *1st strike!*

Later, as personal computers were moving into the mainstream, he attended a conference in the 1970s where operating systems were coming into their own. At the conference, there were 2 presenters: one discussing Linux (Linus Torvalds) and the other discussing how there was plenty of room for multiple platforms. The other, an unkempt, smelly teenager who stated that there was only room for 1 in the market… Bill Gates, who created Microsoft. The potential client chose the former system, Linux. *Strike 2!*

A quick timeline: 1975: The spark. Altair 8800 (1st true PC) is released (Bill Gates/Paul Allen). Microsoft founded. 1977: PCs go mainstream. 1980: Pivotal deal. IBM selects MS for the operating system. 1981: PC standardization: IBM's Model 5150; PC clones explode (Compaq, Dell, + others); MS-DOS as default PC operating system. 1985: Interface leap: MS positioned for mass adoption beyond business users to mainstream consumers. 1986: Microsoft IPO MARCH 13, 1986- my mother's birthday! (Initial public offering).

For context: $10,000 invested in 1986 (assumes reinvestment of dividends, holding, no timing/trading) would be worth approximately $8-10 million today! For a fair comparison, the S&P 500 (a non-managed compilation of 500 stocks) would have been valued at $350- $450,000.

As he sat in my office, he asked whether he should invest in the market or pay off his mortgage. This was a post-crash period where history would identify a possible low. My question to him was: *"What the heck are you doing in my office? You've already missed 2 lightning strike moments in your financial life."* I never heard from him again, and I'm pretty sure he paid off his house.

My simple advice: You can't eat a house, but a house can eat you. Rules of thumb: Pay attention to the margins or spreads between what your cost is for servicing debt vs the potential rate of returns. *Bigger is better here!* Companies and individuals that don't have an ample level of liquidity don't survive crises. It's like water, you don't die right away, but eventually...

Market Sectors

A disciplined approach to investing involves a diversified portfolio, or "pie," across different sectors of the market. For example, stocks, bonds, cash, alternatives, and commodities are all different holdings. The thinking goes like this: Something's up, and others are down, but holding varying pieces evens out the up/downs of the market.

This is a classic example of the win-place-show approach to investing vs. a 1-horse speculative approach.

Stocks, Bonds, Cash and Alternatives

Stocks represent an "ownership" stake in an entity or company. Certain benefits, such as profits, are usually distributed through regular dividend payouts. Also, inherit the capital or purchase amount of a particular stock, which can rise or fall based on the market and the company's performance, or lack of it. Forces of supply and demand, overall economic conditions, and research/development are just a few elements at work that impact a stock.

If stocks are ownership, then bonds are debt or IOU positions that companies, sovereign governments, municipalities, and states can issue. Depending on the type of issuance, these positions are similar to other loans. For example, are the collateralized against assets of the issuer? These are usually considered lower risk and therefore offer lower returns. "Senior" debt is usually near the top of the line in the event the issuer fails. Bonds pay regular dividends/interest and are also referred to as coupon rates, depending on what type of structure they're being paid from (mutual fund/ETF, individual, or municipal bond).

The credit rating of an issuer (borrower) of a bond determines both the issuer's ability to repay you (the lender) and the rate they pay. So, the higher the risk of non-repayment, the higher the borrowing rate, much like an individual loan. Tax treatment varies widely depending on what is being borrowed and who is borrowing. "Junk bonds" tend to pay higher dividends than municipal or government bonds due to the risk of default. Municipal bonds sometimes offer tax-free benefits in some form or another. Often, their payouts are referred to as tax-free equivalent rates.

Cash is, well, cash. Liquid, short-term instruments like savings accounts, money market funds, certificates of deposit, or other time commitment instruments.

Alternatives cover a wide range of investments that are none of the above that use different structures, strategies, and asset classes to generate returns that may offer diversification benefits without correlation with the broad market as a whole.

Commodities

A simple definition of this class is a hard asset (such as oil, gas, gold, silver, or other precious metals). Gold has typically been viewed as a fear/dear asset and bought in response to scenarios such as high sovereign debt levels, potential defaults, and fiat monetary systems (currencies not backed by gold/silver, other than the goodwill/faith of a particular government entity).

Gold/silver's most recent run-up to historically high levels has been based, at least in part, on these very basics. Silver, copper, palladium, and zinc all have industrial applications, and, based on recent AI data center infrastructure demands, there may be a possible shortfall and demand cycle in the near to intermediate future, according to some.

These asset classes tend to rise and fall sharply, so minding the "shop" on these is critical.

Rebalancing is a tool often utilized to maintain the percentage of holdings in each part of the representative "pie." Systematic rebalancing discipline regularly tends to keep portfolios in order and balance. Trading off high/highs for higher lows is the philosophy being applied here.

Market Math

We often ask clients this question: *"If your portfolio drops -50%, what return do you have to make to get back to even?"* Answer: 100%, so don't lose -50%! While this may appear obvious, it is essential to the risk/reward approach to investing and is a stark contrast to speculative investing. Neither is right nor wrong, and should ideally match an individual's risk/reward sentiment.

Professional Analysis and Model Builders

CFAs (Certified Financial Analysts) filter and "build" our trading models that match each risk class. These can be created for mutual funds (professionally managed portfolios with redemption assurances at the end of the market close every day @4:30 pm EST), ETFs (Exchange Traded Funds-*enhanced index funds that aren't managed typically at a lower cost and trade like a stock within market trading hours)*, stocks, and bonds. We prefer ETFs for their lower fees, sector purity, and tactical trading qualities.

The potential advantage is ensuring the purity of methodology, as fund managers can and do experience "style drift." Simply put, they chase returns to enhance reporting and deviate from their stated philosophical categories.

I liken it to a baseball batting lineup. A team needs players who represent single, double, and home run hitters to balance out the order. If the single hitter starts swinging like a home run hitter, there may be no one on base and fewer runs. While good home run hitters hit them out of the park more often, they also statistically strike out at a greater rate than the other types of batters. You don't need that to happen in your portfolio either.

EQUITY

Investment Style			Average Market Capitalization
Value	*Blend*	*Growth*	
Large-Cap Value	Large-Cap Blend	Large-Cap Growth	Large
Mid-Cap Value	Mid-Cap Blend	Mid-Cap Growth	Medium
Small-Cap Value	Small-Cap Blend	Small-Cap Growth	Small

Download the "Wealth Waves Analytics Tool" and all the resources from this book at: *WealthWaveTools.com*

Cryptocurrencies: Bitcoin Example

I will begin by saying that one of the most volatile of the investment classes is currencies. It is not for the faint of heart, as market movements tend to be fast and furious.

What does crypto/Bitcoin do? At its core, Bitcoin enables the transfer of value between individuals anywhere in the world using nothing more than a computer and an internet connection.

Why is this revolutionary? Unlike other methods of sending money over the internet, Bitcoin operates without requiring trust in an intermediary. There is no bank, corporation, or centralized authority operating between sender and receiver. As a result, Bitcoin represents the world's first public digital payments infrastructure—public meaning accessible to all and owned by no single entity.

We already rely on public infrastructure for information exchange. Websites, email, and digital communication operate atop the internet, which is itself a public network. In contrast, the only truly public payment infrastructure before Bitcoin was physical cash, which works only for face-to-face transactions.

Before Bitcoin, remote payments made over the phone or the internet could not occur using public infrastructure. Instead, individuals depended on private banks to record transactions internally by debiting one account and crediting another. If the sender and recipient used different banks, the process required multiple institutions, multiple ledgers, and layers of intermediation.

Bitcoin fundamentally changes this model. Its ledger—the blockchain—is public, transparent, and globally accessible. Anyone may add an entry to this ledger by transferring bitcoin to another party. Moreover, anyone—regardless of nationality, race, religion, gender, sex, or creditworthiness—can create a Bitcoin address at no cost and receive digital payments.

In this sense, Bitcoin is the world's first globally accessible public money.

Is it perfect? No. Neither was email when it was first introduced in 1972.

Bitcoin is not superior to existing forms of money in every dimension. It is not universally accepted, prices are rarely denominated in it, and it is not always a stable store of value. Yet it works. And the fact that it functions without trusted intermediaries is extraordinary. Bitcoin represents a breakthrough in computer science—one that may ultimately prove as consequential for freedom, prosperity, and human flourishing as the invention of the internet itself.

Importantly, Bitcoin is only the beginning. If private payment infrastructure can be replaced with public alternatives, then other privately controlled choke points in human interaction may also be re-architected.

The Problem of Centralized Failure

Systems with single points of failure are inherently vulnerable. Whether that point of failure is a corporation or a government is immaterial; no critical infrastructure should depend on one centralized authority.

Similar choke points existed before the Internet. To disseminate information, one had to pass through a handful of television broadcasters or newspapers. While private corporations play a vital role in society, no essential infrastructure should rely on only one or two dominant actors.

This raises an important question: Why should societies invest in public infrastructure? Why should blockchains be favored over corporate intermediaries? Why tolerate their inefficiencies and work to improve them? And why should the pioneers of this technology remain in the United States rather than relocating abroad?

The answer is straightforward. The corporate intermediaries that provide today's privately owned but systemically critical infrastructure are becoming fewer in number, larger in scale, and more powerful in influence. As they consolidate, the consequences of their failures grow increasingly severe.

This argument does not rely on claims of price appreciation, mass adoption timelines, or speculative upside. It is grounded almost entirely in architectural concerns: the fragility created by concentrated intermediaries, the risks posed by opaque infrastructure, and the systemic consequences of single points of failure.

Lessons from Recent Failures

Markets and policymakers have been repeatedly reminded of how dependent modern systems are on centralized platforms:

- Major cloud service outages have taken large portions of the internet offline.

- Software supply-chain compromises have cascaded across governments and enterprises.
- Disruptions to critical infrastructure have spilled over into the real world, affecting economic activity.
- High-profile financial failures have exposed the risks of opaque custody and centralized control.

Blockchains caused none of these failures. Yet taken together, they reinforce the underlying concern: When essential systems quietly consolidate, their failures scale rapidly and unpredictably.

A Modest but Durable Proposition

This is not an argument that Bitcoin replaces banks, eliminates intermediaries entirely, or resolves broad social challenges. Rather, it advances a more restrained—and therefore more durable—claim: that open, neutral infrastructure for transferring value may reduce certain forms of systemic fragility, much as the internet reduced fragility in communication.

In that sense, Bitcoin should be understood not as a cure-all, but as a foundational innovation—one that challenges how societies design, govern, and safeguard the systems upon which they depend.

A Platform Proactive Approach for Employer Sponsored Plans

Employer-sponsored plans can be directed and managed on the same platform vs. "buy/hope." As a professional with discretionary authorization, our ability to manage on an existing platform is based on the funds available within the plan to build at least 3 distinctive models: conservative, moderate, and growth. A limitation characteristic, like the frequency of trade rules of the particular plan, must be considered, because they almost always limit trades as compared to a personal account and platform.

In-service-withdrawals (ISW) vary by plan administration structure, and it's common to have the right to roll out (IRS rules prefer institution to institution) entire balances or employee contributions at age 59.5 into a self-directed IRA. These are not taxable to the employee, and investment options and control can improve dramatically.

Whether you're doing this yourself or with professional wealth management, investment positions/tools, in addition to trading capabilities, should expand to include everything available, rather than limited choices via employer plans. As professional wealth managers, we prefer this setup.

So, it's *good* to have employer-sponsored plans because of the disciplined payroll deduction savings.

It's even *better* if the employer matches contributions on some level.

It's preferred to have all options and unrestricted trade capability to take advantage of fluid market opportunities and to avoid major downtrends and perils of the market.

Market Cycles Philosophy

There is a cycle for capital, and a strategy
for every market condition.

A time to invest, and a time to deploy cash; a time
to buy conviction, and a time to take profits.

A time for stocks, and a time for bonds; a time
to seek growth, a time to preserve capital.

A time for momentum, and a time for fundamentals; a
time to respond to outcomes, and a time to respect causes.

A time to allocate; and a time to reassess; a time
to act decisively, and a time to stay patient.

What return comes to any investor who
ignores the tides of the market?

KEY TAKEAWAYS

- Markets rarely behave the way simple supply-and-demand logic suggests; when a trade looks "too obvious," forces like "priced in" often flip the script.
- Professional traders profit in anticipation, buying the rumor and selling the news long before the crowd reacts.
- Sentiment indicators like the AAII survey show that when most investors are euphoric or terrified, the smart money is usually on the other side.
- Even elite hedge fund managers only win slightly more than half the time, revealing that pure animal instincts drive much of what happens in the market.
- Index funds outperform many professionals for one simple reason: they have no emotions, no fear, and no impulse to hold too long or bail too soon.
- Win, place, or show is a risk/reward-balanced approach vs. a more speculative 1-horse approach.
- Riding the markets up/down by buying/holding can be less effective than strategically repositioning to the trends/tides of market movements.
- Winnings aren't winnings unless you take some off the table.
- Improve your chances by using platforms with components and rules that enable independent management.
- Stop guessing and start measuring results as a process.

Your IPAs (Not the Beer)

Write your *Identify Plan Actions* here:

IDENTIFIED item(s):

PLAN (your strategy):

ACTIONS (take a step forward):

4

Element Two: Tax Efficiency

Paying taxes may be inevitable; however, the amount is to be determined.

Let me begin by saying that I'm very proud to be an American. A part of that is certainly paying taxes. I also feel like it's my patriotic duty to pay as little as I legally and possibly can to remain financially viable, independent, and self-sufficient. That way, we can support our families, our communities, charities, and those who are in need and less fortunate.

Paying taxes historically is as old as our country itself – it's actually older. Being a student of history, I'm uncertain whether there was ever a period in human existence when we didn't pay taxes in some form or another. I'm pretty sure that after God made man on the sixth day, he may have created a gray area for taxes to exist. In fact, our entire country was born, in part, from a desire to be free and not to be unduly taxed. Patrick Henry's declaration, "Give me liberty or give me death," certainly embodies that sentiment. The fiery desire for freedom from tyranny and from being unduly taxed was the very impetus of the Revolutionary War and the birth of our Republic.

Regardless of the political structure (monarchy, dictatorship, democracy, or constitutional republic), humans seem to have a desire to keep more of the fruits of our own labor. If a government of whatever form is good at anything, it certainly is really good at spending other people's money. Income tax, as we know, began in 1913 and was two pages on one piece of paper, front and back. The tax law itself was not much more than that, and it has since exploded. It has become an actual cottage industry of preparation and also planning for tax avoidance. If you recall, the notorious gangster Al Capone did not go to prison for all of his alleged illegal activities, but rather for income evasion. Income avoidance, on the other hand, is completely 100% legal.

Tax Story

In all of the public speaking I've done over my career, I would request," Please raise your hand if you feel like you're not paying your fair share of taxes yet." The only ones to do so were messing with me or not paying attention. The one exception I experienced was the man who raised his hand and responded that if he was paying more tax, then he must be making money!

While there is certainly some truth to that, it's generally a good idea not to volunteer to pay taxes on money you're not spending today.

You are robbing yourself of the triple compounding factor...interest on principle, interest on interest, and interest on deferred taxes!

The differences between tax preparation and tax planning are immense. I liken the contrast between preparers and planners to toll roads and bypasses. Whether you are using tax preparation through a franchise provider or software, a professional CPA, or whoever, their training is all the same. Follow the rules: look for the red lights, stop signs, speed limits, and don't deviate. Planners know the laws and rules; however, they identify and develop strategies to minimize, defer, and avoid unnecessary taxation. Instead of taking the "toll road," they choose the bypass, highways, and roundabouts (I love these as long as people know how to navigate them).

Diversification

Good planning involves all three categories of tax planning: taxable, tax-deferred, and tax-free. All of these have distinct characteristics, benefits, and trade-offs.

For example, *taxable* investments have something called cost basis. The original amount or principal that was invested represents the starting point from which all gains and losses are calculated for income tax purposes. The gains are typically deferred until the position is actually sold. A few benefits are that you can sell it at a time that suits your situation. When you have losses, you can do the same and use tax-harvesting strategies, selling the losers to offset the gains from winners. Dividends are typically taxed as they are received and add to the cost basis, reducing the taxable amount when they are sold.

Tax-deferred accounts can benefit from compounding because gains accrue on the principal, accrued interest, and deferred taxes. This fits the rule of not paying tax on money you're not using today. On the flip side, withdrawals are currently taxed at ordinary income tax (OIT) rates rather than the long-term capital gains rate, which is usually lower than OIT.

Tax-free accounts are those that are not subject to tax when sold.

Tax law covers a wide variety of special-interest incentives to encourage self-sufficiency, such as qualified savings plans like IRAs, Roth IRAs, backdoor IRAs, 401(k)s, 403(b)s (non-profits), and tax-deferred compensation, to name a few. The incentives are obviously to get us to save for our own retirement. Some of these offer tax deductions on contributions on the front side, and the contributions are taxed when they are withdrawn. Other plans, like Roth IRAs, are designed with taxes paid up front, with a promise of tax-free distributions upon distribution.

What belies all of this is the question of w*hat taxes will be in the future,* which is certainly unknown. Other incentivized tax laws, such as those in the real estate industry, have led to the creation of 1031 exchanges. These allow someone to trade up in their real estate holdings by rolling over their gains into a new property or holding that is worth more than the previous one. Deferring capital gains takes many forms and comes in various shapes and sizes. It is often credited to Albert Einstein, who said, "*Compound interest is the eighth wonder of the world.*" So interest on the principal, interest on the interest, and interest on deferred taxes are inevitably powerful tools for creating wealth. A good general rule is not to pay tax on money you're not using today.

Now, the argument could be made that if death taxes are inevitable, why bother deferring them? Think of the ultimate tax bill due like a mortgage, which is typical for home purchases. It is sometimes said that what is being created cannot ultimately be avoided in someone's estate. Currently, the federal estate tax exclusion is nearly $15 million per person. Couples are exempt from $30 million. In addition, the annual limit for gifts to anyone you wish is $19,000 per individual.

Another strategy I've seen applied, in addition to deferring and avoiding the tax currently, is to purchase a life insurance policy that will pay the income taxes ultimately due. The premiums can be gifted to pay the premiums if structured under a trust. These strategies are referred to as utilizing "discounted dollars" because the amount paid for death proceeds vs. premiums is less than the tax itself at a considerably lower cost.

Capital gains can be offset in a strategy known as "tax loss harvesting." Simply put, sell losing positions (assuming they aren't likely to recover) against winners to lessen the tax due. The insurance industry also has some tax advantages under current laws and through lobbying for its products. *Word of caution: Watch for the expenses as they can eat up the benefits.*

While most death benefits are free of income tax, they can increase the estate inheritance tax. Under certain circumstances, an older life insurance or annuity policy can be 1035 exchanged for a newer policy with additional benefits. There are specific rules for these "rollover" type strategies that must be adhered to to achieve the desired outcome.

Tax Strategic Planning represents an approach and a collection of tools that, if utilized by a skilled individual, can yield significant outcomes. If misapplied by amateurs, it can cause considerable damage. The more there is at risk, the more likely it is to utilize a professional to achieve your goals.

The tax laws themselves are subject to change, so the strategies must adapt to the shifting environment of tax avoidance. I've often found it useful for my clients, as well as for me, to seek out and hire professionals who deal with "like circumstances" because it's second nature to them. They don't have to stop what they're doing and go look it up and figure out how to apply it. Most of the time, we don't have the luxury or the money to waste on somebody's learning curve.

While this chapter is not intended to be a comprehensive guide to tax efficiency, it is meant to pique the interest of those seeking to identify and take advantage of potential benefits for wealth creation and retention. Happy hunting!

Download the "Wealth Waves Tax Efficiency Checklist" and all the resources from this book at: *WealthWaveTools.com*

Recap

Taxes are inevitable, but how much you pay — and when — is often a choice made through planning. The American tax system is designed not only to collect revenue but also to encourage specific behaviors: saving, investing, owning property, and supporting family and community. *Knowing how to read between the lines of that incentive structure is the art of tax efficiency.* The key distinction is this: tax preparation looks backward and reports what happened;

tax planning looks forward and engineers what *will* happen. Smart use of incentives, deferrals, exchanges, and offsets creates a financial roadmap that keeps more of your money working for you — legally, ethically, and strategically. Tax efficiency is not about dodging responsibility; it's about honoring the rules while refusing to play the game blindly. Professionals who understand the ever-changing code can find the bypasses that lead to wealth preservation and generational impact.

Tax Efficiency Wisdom

What does it profit any investor to achieve gains only to lose them to taxes?

KEY TAKEAWAYS

- Taxes are inevitable, but the amount you pay is largely determined by strategy. Preparation looks backward, while planning engineers for the future.
- The tax code is full of incentives designed to reward saving, investing, owning property, and being financially self-sufficient; knowing how to use those incentives keeps more of your money working for you.
- On money you're not spending today, leverage the 3x compounding rule.
- Tools like IRAs, Roth IRAs, 401(k)s, 1031 and 1035 exchanges, tax-loss harvesting, and discounted-dollar insurance strategies can defer, reduce, or offset taxes when used correctly.
- Misapplied tax strategies can do real harm, which is why professionals who work with "like circumstances" are essential; they know the bypasses, not just the toll roads.
- Don't think of tax efficiency as avoiding responsibility. Learn to navigate the system intelligently, adapt as laws change, and preserve wealth across your lifetime and beyond.

Your IPAs

➔ **Implementation:** Identify and catalog all tax-advantaged accounts and tools currently in use — IRAs, Roth IRAs, 401(k)s, HSAs, 529 plans, charitable vehicles, real estate exchanges, and insurance contracts. Confirm how each aligns with your short-, mid-, and long-term objectives.

➔ **Planning:** Model potential future tax environments and estimate your lifetime effective tax rate. Explore conversions, deferrals, and harvesting strategies that reduce taxes across decades rather than years. Integrate estate-planning strategies — gifting, trusts, and discounted-dollar insurance — into your overall plan. Action: Coordinate with your advisory team — financial planner, CPA, attorney — to implement and document each strategy. Schedule annual "tax efficiency audits" to ensure current rules and thresholds are applied (gift limits, contribution caps, income phase-outs, etc.).

➔ **Accountability:** Review outcomes each year:

- What was deferred or saved?
- How did those savings compound?
- Did legislative changes alter any assumptions?

Keep clear, measurable benchmarks. Tax planning should evolve just as the tax laws and your life do.

Your IPAs (Not the Beer)

Write your *Identify Plan Actions* here:

IDENTIFIED item(s):

PLAN (your strategy):

ACTIONS (take a step forward):

5

Element Three: Protection

Only buy insurance to cover what you don't want to write a check for...

This chapter is about protecting the wealth you've worked hard to accumulate—both as you build it and once you've achieved your goals. We'll also explore how to transfer risk appropriately, especially when the financial consequence would be catastrophic. Most often, this means utilizing insurance or a similar strategy.

"I hate insurance!"

That's what one man told me when I first entered the financial services industry over four decades ago. At the time, I was surprised by his reaction. But looking back, I realized what he meant: *he resented the idea of paying premiums for something he hoped he would never use.* In essence, he didn't want to write a check for something intangible, even if it offered protection. He may have considered himself self-insured, but in truth, he was stuck between a rock and a hard place.

A better approach is to accept higher deductibles (risk) and find the "sweet spot" in the resulting premium reductions. For example, if electing a $1000 deductible reduces your premium by 50%, but a $2000 deductible only reduces it 55%, choose the first reduction because your potential loss would be another $950 out of pocket. Then, calculate how many years it would take to break even. This works for all insurance. Save and invest the difference, and you'll have it available just in case you do experience a loss and fun money if you don't!

I am very proactive in my health and fitness, and in overall risk management, and I adjust my deductibles accordingly. When driving, I utilize the rule "9 you're fine, 10 you're mine" for speed limits. In parking lots (a very risky place), my head is on a swivel, and I "pull straight through" or back into a space to minimize the risk of running into someone else's vehicle or person.

Note: If you don't "sell" the risk off to another party (insurance company, etc.), you ARE self-insured!

When analyzing risk, this would be catastrophic. Take homeowners' insurance, for example. The odds of your home burning down or being destroyed are low, but the cost to rebuild can be financially devastating. Even if your mortgage is paid off, would you really want to save a few hundred or thousand dollars a year only to risk losing your home entirely? Likely not.

On the flip side, when the risk is minor, it may make more sense to retain it. Every time I'm at an electronics store and asked if I want to buy an extended warranty or protection plan, my answer is almost always no. The cost of the replacement is usually close to the cost of the plan itself—and in many cases, the manufacturer's warranty is sufficient. I performed a simple math exercise: How many years to break even? Simply, the cost of the purchased item to replace is divided by the insurance outlay, considering the "life expectancy" of the product.

The other exercise is to list the "risk item" on the left side of the ledger and access/apply a "loss" number (1-10) on the right side. Losses can be physical, financial, mental, or emotional. The closer the total gets to 10, the more you might consider purchasing some form of protection.

It's always wise to mitigate risks where possible. A simple example: when parking, I try to pull through so I can exit the space headfirst. This small habit reduces the risk of backing into someone or something. While riding my motorcycle, skydiving, or scuba diving, I am defensive in my behavior to survive by wearing bright yellow, double- and triple-checking my equipment, and not drinking alcohol before or during these activities.

Another principle: avoid risks that are both catastrophic and uninsurable. For instance, while I enjoy watching storm chasing shows on TV, I have no intention of ever chasing tornadoes myself.

A Social Security Insurance Story

While you may not think of Social Security as an insurance plan per se, it actually is. It was created in 1935 under the FDR administration, with the first retirement benefits beginning in January 1940. It was initiated as an old workers' benefit to lure the aging "missionary generation" out so that the younger workers, "lost generation," could have jobs during the depression. As time went on, disability, Medicare/Medicaid, survivors' benefits, and other benefits were added.

I had a couple of friends (not clients) who didn't plan for their retirement benefits. They had both been divorced and then remarried to each other without considering the huge impact on their benefits.

Once, while sharing a meal, the wife was discussing her retirement plans, looking forward to it, and drawing on her former husband's benefits. As the rules dictate, if one was married for at least 10 years, currently unmarried, at least 62 years of age, and has been divorced for at least 2 years, she could claim, even if her previous spouse wasn't drawing.

I asked her point-blank: Aren't you and (current spouse) legally married after your first divorce? Yes? You will now be drawing off of the second husband's benefits because they had been married for over 10 years. Unfortunately, her first husband had a significantly higher reportable income than her second husband, who had been creatively skirting taxes for a number of years and was affecting both of their future benefits. She didn't speak to me for some time after this revelation. It *pays out in spades to know the rules and applications* for insurance of all kinds.

Another couple, also friends of both us and the aforementioned couple, were contemplating marriage as they were both divorced. While I was not providing spiritual/moral guidance, I informed the bride-to-be that she would sacrifice a significant income benefit if she were legally married.

She has been eternally grateful for the financial advice that I provided her and maintains her financial independence and relationship without the legal status.

> *This testimonial was given by a former client of Rik Saylor Financial. No cash or non-cash compensation was paid or promised in exchange for this testimonial, and the client has no other material conflict of interest in providing it. The client's experience may not be representative of the experience of other clients. Past performance is not indicative of future results, and this testimonial is not a guarantee of any particular outcome.*

Understanding Shared Risk

It helps to visualize how insurance works. Picture a large bucket—at the top are all the people contributing premiums. This bucket represents the insurance company. As claims come in, money flows out through a spigot at the bottom. This pooling of resources spreads out the cost of loss so no single individual bears the full financial brunt. Shared risk isn't a new concept—it's been around for centuries, possibly even millennia.

Property and casualty insurance is a good example. If you drive a car or own property, you're often legally required to carry insurance. Insurers use underwriting to assess risk factors such as age, gender, behavior, location, and the value of the insured asset, as well as collective losses in a given area. For example, young male drivers under age 25 typically pay more for auto insurance—not because of their specific behavior, but because statistically, they are more likely to be involved in accidents.

When I was 23, my car insurance premiums were high. But when I turned 25, they dropped significantly because I was now rated on how I used the car, not just my age.

Other risk factors include where you live. If your area has a high number of insurance claims, your premiums will reflect that. Likewise, driving a high-performance vehicle increases your premiums, as the potential payout/loss is much higher.

NOTE: It pays to shop insurance carriers every couple of years because of these factors.

The same logic applies to life insurance. Premiums are based on age, health history, family history, and behaviors such as smoking, scuba diving, or skydiving.

A personal example: A few years ago, I purchased a life insurance policy with an accelerated death benefit. If I become critically, chronically, or terminally ill, I can tap into the policy during my lifetime. I disclosed a history of high cholesterol and received a 25% surcharge. I asked the underwriter if the surcharge could be removed if I improved my numbers. They agreed to review it.

Two years later, I had successfully lowered my cholesterol—but I had taken up scuba diving, which added a different 25% surcharge. Our behaviors can increase or decrease risk, and premiums are adjusted accordingly.

Health and Long-Term Care Risk

Let me begin by saying that our personal behaviors, beyond inherited genetics, are our best "insurance." Proper sleep, diet, and exercise can mitigate the vast majority of health issues. I'm fond of saying, "I may have inherited my genetics, but all of the maintenance is up to me!"

Health risks are some of the most significant we face. One serious medical event can wipe out a lifetime of savings. Most people are covered by a major medical group or individual health insurance until Medicare begins at age 65. If one spouse is still working, it's not uncommon to keep a retired spouse covered under major medical, which nearly always offers better coverage and pricing. These plans often include deductibles and co-insurance—both forms of shared risk.

When I began in this industry 43 years ago, one in four people didn't live to see age 65. That means 75% did. In my own family, I've seen the opposite. Of my three brothers, all passed before 65. I have outlived all of my siblings at this point, and God willing, will outlive both of my parents, who passed at 74 and 75.

Research suggests that disability and long-term care needs are common financial risks that many individuals and couples may face during their lifetimes. Planning in advance can help address the potential financial impact of these events.

I view long-term care insurance as portfolio protection. *If you don't transfer this risk, you are self-insured.* If care costs $100,000 to

$300,000 a year, that comes directly out of your pocket, most likely with taxable funds.

Long-term care benefits are typically triggered by the inability to perform two out of six activities of daily living (e.g., bathing, dressing, toileting). Older policies often required nursing home confinement, but newer policies are more flexible. A drawback of traditional policies is that they can become prohibitively more expensive as you age.

In my own case, I chose a policy with a $1 million death benefit that allows me to draw up to 24% per year for 4 years if I need care on an indemnity (vs. cost reimbursement) basis and tax-free. Also, my location doesn't matter, whether I'm at home (my preference) or in a semi- or full-care facility.

In many cases, life insurance death benefits are received by beneficiaries free of federal income tax. For most policies, once coverage is issued, the insurer (company) cannot cancel the policy as long as premiums are paid, and the premium is typically fixed by the policy terms. This depends on the type of policy and the contract provisions.

These types of policies are underwritten for mortality and morbidity risks (death and illness). My breakeven on my own policy is over 60 years(in non-inflation-adjusted dollars). Calculating the number of years I will pay in vs. the amount paid out, whether I need assistance or a death payout. I'm counting on innovation in the delivery of medical services and efficiency to make up the difference.

> *Insurance and annuity products, as well as risk-management strategies, involve costs (including premiums, mortality and expense charges, rider costs, and surrender charges), limitations, exclusions, and conditions that vary by product, carrier, and jurisdiction. Any guarantees associated with an insurance or annuity product are backed solely by the claims-paying ability and financial strength of the issuing insurance company and are not FDIC insured or bank guaranteed. Insurance and annuity products are not suitable for every person or situation, may have tax consequences if modified or surrendered, and should be evaluated against an individual's objectives, time horizon, liquidity needs, and risk tolerance. Readers should review product prospectuses or disclosure documents and consult a licensed insurance professional before purchasing, exchanging, or surrendering any insurance or annuity product.*

Download the "Wealth Waves Insurance Cheat Sheet: Basic Rules of Risk Management" and all the resources from this book at: *WealthWaveTools.com*

The Role of Innovation

As aging baby boomers enter the healthcare system, innovation is inevitable. Need, as they say, is the mother of invention. One silver lining from the COVID pandemic was the rapid expansion of telemedicine. These advances, along with the rise of nurse practitioners, are helping meet the exploding demand. The same baby boom wave that drove up personal consumption expenditures has shifted forward, as demographics show that, from age 50 onward, we spend more on healthcare for the remainder of our lives.

The digital age we live in continues to deliver amazing technologies that can remotely and in real time measure a wide range of conditions.

Choosing an Insurance Provider

When choosing an insurance carrier, I evaluate:

- Financial stability (via AM Best, Moody's, etc.)
- Claims-paying reputation/service
- Competitiveness of their specific product(s)

I recommend working with a knowledgeable insurance professional. DIY resources exist, but a licensed expert can help navigate the nuances and complexities of this maze.

Download the "Wealth Waves Insurance Provider Ratings" and all the resources from this book at: *WealthWaveTools.com*

In Summary

We must regularly assess the risks in our lives and decide what we want to retain and what we want to transfer. It takes a lifetime to build wealth—and one moment to lose it.

For business owners and high-net-worth individuals, especially, extra layers of protection, such as professional liability insurance and umbrella policies, are essential.

Umbrella coverage can be a relatively low-cost way to increase liability protection beyond your underlying auto or homeowners limits. For example, if an auto policy provides $500,000 of liability coverage, the umbrella policy may increase the total protection to $2-3 million for an additional premium, depending on the insurer, your risk profile, and required underlying limits.

Your challenge is to identify the gaps. How much risk are you willing to keep—and how much are you willing to pay to avoid writing a check when something goes wrong?

It's a risk/reward evaluation worth revisiting often.

KEY TAKEAWAYS

- Protection planning involves deciding which risks you can afford to keep and which could be catastrophic enough to transfer to an insurer. (Loss cost)
- Minor risks can be self-insured, but major risks, such as health events, long-term care, and liability exposure, can wipe out a lifetime of savings/assets if not appropriately transferred.
- Know the rules and applications of insurance and utilize them wisely.
- Find the sweet spot for premium efficiency and invest the savings.
- Insurance works through shared risk, where underwriting evaluates your behaviors, insured behaviors, location, loss ratios, age, and health to determine premiums that match your true exposure.
- Using insurance to cover certain risks can mean you don't need to keep as much cash set aside. That may free up money for other FUN GOALS!
- Health, long-term care, and life insurance strategies evolve with innovation, and choosing the right carrier and structure often requires a seasoned professional who understands the nuances. *Protection is only as viable as the insurance company itself.*
- Building wealth takes decades, but losing it can happen in a moment. Regularly reviewing your coverage and identifying gaps will preserve what you've worked so hard to create.

Your IPAs (Not the Beer)

Write your *Identify Plan Actions* here:

IDENTIFIED item(s):

PLAN (your strategy):

ACTIONS (take a step forward):

6

Element Four: Legacy, Chaos, and the Choice to Plan

Plan for your demise because none of us are getting out of here alive!

Death and taxes anchor life's certainties, yet in estate planning there is a third: the need for a clean dismount. Just as a gymnast is judged by how they land, our financial lives are ultimately measured by how well we transfer what we've built. We can accumulate wisely, manage well, reduce taxes, and protect our assets, yet still fail the final handoff. That final transfer is the dismount, and it's where many legacies break apart.

After 43 years in financial services and having recently served as administrator of my late brother's estate, I've seen the consequences of poor planning firsthand.

Freedom from Stuff

Nobody really wants your stuff. What they want are the memories of you. Ok, well, certainly the items with intrinsic real market value.

The good, the bad, and the ugly of decluttering is that it may be the most loving act—and the greatest gift—you can give to those you leave behind.

There is a simple rule I strive to live by: If you haven't used it or needed it recently, it needs to go. My favorite mental trap is "I might need this someday." When that day finally arrives, I can't find the item anyway. I go to the store, buy a replacement, and only later discover the original—neatly stored, forgotten, and useless. Sad but true.

Both of my parents were children of the Great Depression. My siblings and I were raised with the "waste not, want not" philosophy deeply ingrained in our thinking. That value still matters to me. I continue to resist waste and inefficiency wherever possible. I strive to be a good steward of all that has been entrusted to me.

But I've also learned that there is freedom in letting go. Letting go of the belief that I must cling to things I might need someday. Letting go of the fear that releasing possessions is irresponsible. Trusting instead that God will provide what I truly need when the time comes. An abundance mentality replacing the scarcity mentality of my upbringing.

And recognizing this truth: Someone, somewhere, can use it right now.

To ease my concern about waste, I turn to organizations that exist for exactly this purpose—Goodwill, AMVETS, churches, food and clothing outreach programs, the Salvation Army, and others. These channels allow usefulness to continue beyond me.

Grief is hard enough. Sorting through the accumulated possessions of a lifetime—while grieving—is something no one should have to endure unnecessarily. As the administrator of my late brother's estate, and as the last remaining immediate family member, I experienced probate firsthand. I saw clearly what my heirs might one day face if I did not change course.

The "merit badge" experience of settling his estate is one I would never wish upon myself—or anyone else—again. Negotiating with estate vultures was exhausting and demoralizing. Because my other two deceased brothers each had two children, the per stirpes distribution rule for intestate(no will or trust) went into effect. I felt obligated to extract every possible dollar on their behalf because it could potentially have a profound impact on their lives. After fifteen months of probate-related struggles, I finally found closure—but not without cost.

That experience changed me.

While the heirs praised and thanked me for my efforts and the eventual outcome, the pain lingered from the entire ordeal and could have been avoided if my brother had done some planning. It compelled me to urge others to get their houses in order—literally and figuratively. Physically. Financially. Legally. Estate documents included. This is not administrative busywork. It is an ultimate act of love for the people you care about most. I am thankful for the team of professionals I encountered: estate attorneys, estate appraisers/auctioneers, and professional resources.

Western civilization seems to have traded spiritual depth for material accumulation, leaving us poorer. Our families, our cities, our country—and our world—would be better served by returning our focus to what truly matters. Our relationships while we are alive and far beyond our passing from this world to the next.

Spoiler alert: You can't take it with you—no matter how much your heirs might wish you would!

Download "The Ten Truths to Declutter Guide" and all the resources from this book at: ***WealthWaveTools.com***

Why Probate Happens

A deceased person cannot legally own assets. Anything with a title, such as financial accounts, real estate, and vehicles, must be transferred, often through probate. Probate is time-consuming, administrative, and frequently inefficient.

My brother passed in May 2024 without a will. He died intestate, so the court appointed me as administrator. His estate had to be distributed per stirpes (living bloodline). I was one of four brothers. Two had passed earlier, each leaving two children. Their shares are divided among their kids.

As the court-appointed administrator, I needed signatures from five heirs for major transactions involving the home, the vehicle, and the construction equipment, and I had to submit everything to the court. While frustrating, the accountability made sense. Without a designated executor, the court stepped in. I believe my brother assumed I'd "just handle it" because of my profession. I love and miss him, but when I see him again, I'm going to fake a high five and return the gut punch!

What Most People Get Wrong

Many adults either lack a written estate plan or haven't updated it to reflect their current circumstances. If you don't care what happens after you're gone, do nothing. But your heirs may likely face confusion, conflict, and extra cost. Estate planning is emotionally difficult, but far easier than leaving chaos behind.

In my case, things worked out because I could be bonded, I lived in the state, and all heirs agreed to let me handle the process. Still, my brother tried to protect assets by forming a poorly drafted irrevocable trust. One attorney with thirty years of estate experience called it one of the worst he'd seen. We had to hire counsel just to unwind it.

Download "Misconceptions About Estate Planning" and all the resources from this book at: *WealthWaveTools.com*

A Better Solution: The Revocable Living Trust

A Revocable Living Trust is a common tool that can help assets pass outside of probate. This varies by state, the assets involved, and your specific goals. You retitle assets into the trust while you are alive, so nothing needs to be transferred after your death. You remain in control as the trustee and can amend the trust at any time (revocable). After death, your successor trustee steps in and follows your instructions.

I explain it like operating a vehicle. You're driving. Your spouse is the front-seat passenger and is likely the next potential driver. Successor trustees sit in the back. Every asset that is titled, including your home(s), vehicles, and accounts, is placed into the trunk. When you pass, the next person moves into the driver's seat, avoiding probate, public record, and possible delays.

NOTE: You don't have to "own" the asset in order to control it. In this way, your assets have been "transferred " out of your name and into the trust, avoiding the expensive and time-consuming process of changing ownership names after your death.

In states like Ohio, properly executed trusts avoid probate and protect privacy.

A proper trust package includes a Revocable Living Trust, a Pour-Over Will (for assets without title: furniture, personal possessions), a Durable Financial Power of Attorney, a Healthcare Power of Attorney, and a Living Will. These last 2 are commonly referred to as Medical Directives.

One Attorney Experience

In my many years of seeing estates and the train wreck effect outcomes, I've also observed a wide range of attorneys and their respective approaches, both proactive and reactive. As one attorney said to me, "If your estate goes through probate, don't worry, we won't charge you that much!" My response was, "Why would my estate pay anything that it didn't need to pay in the first place if it could avoid it?!"

I wondered, do they fund the pond of derelict estates the probate attorneys fish from?

I was working with an attorney who focused solely on probate-avoidance planning in his practice. He told me about a time when he was instructing a class for CE credits for attorneys, and at the break, he was approached. The attorney said to him," Don't you realize you are cutting your own throat by avoiding probate?!"

The cost can vary widely depending on the complexity of your estate, the manner in which it will be distributed to beneficiaries, and the way they will receive it (all at once or incrementally at different amounts/ages). I have seen Revocable Living Trusts and accompanying documents cost $2,500-$10,000. While I'm not an attorney, the difference appeared to originate from where the attorney providing the services was, downtown vs. suburban office locations.

A Funding Story

During a break at one of my many public speaking events, a senior couple approached me with a question after my segment on legacy and estate planning. They began by proudly stating that they had completed their Revocable Living Trusts, Financial POAs, Health Care POAs, and Living Wills.

I congratulated them on their thoughtfulness and the hard work I knew was involved in completing this major milestone. I then asked them if they had "funded" their respective trusts, to which they responded that they weren't sure.

The litmus test, I said, is to look at their non-IRA (non-Qualified) type accounts, investment account statements, and property deeds and see whether they are titled in the name of their trusts or in their own names. They replied that their attorney had not recommended performing this because they were "too young." When I asked if they didn't mind, I asked what their ages were; they said 76 & 78! I retorted, "So your attorney sold you trust, and will likely take your estate through probate too!"

My final remark was that if they provided the attorney's name, I would make sure I didn't refer anyone to him! The difference between salespeople and planners.

In my experience, some estate planning attorneys not only draft the trust documents *but also assist with* the actual funding (by transferring assets by retitling them into the trust, where appropriate). They will also coordinate with your financial advisors, insurance providers, etc., to ensure the end result is complete and fulfilled.

Industry studies indicate that a substantial percentage of adults either do not have a written estate plan or have not updated their existing plan. It pays to keep your plan up to date for the benefit of your loved ones.

Common Pitfalls

Unfunded trusts: A number of couples have told me proudly they have a trust, but never titled assets into it. Their trusts will have accomplished nothing to avoid probate.

Improper titles: If your tax bills for real estate or account statements still show your personal name or tenants in common, assets are not properly titled in the trust's name.

Planning for unfit heirs: If an heir isn't ready to manage wealth, you can stagger distributions at different ages, in different manners, amounts, and times. It's compassionate control.

Other Tools

TOD (Transfer on Death) and POD(Paid on Death) designations work well for certain accounts. Larger estates may use strategies like Family Limited Partnerships.

A Cautionary Tale

A couple granted their adult child power of attorney before vacation. When they returned, all assets were liquidated, and the adult child acted legally, albeit not morally or ethically. Choose Financial POA (Power of Attorney) agents wisely.

Many plans should offer a no-contest clause. Someone can still sue, but they risk receiving a token amount like 100$. The estate must defend itself, and legal costs reduce the inheritance for all beneficiaries.

Final Thoughts

Many people who inherit money deplete it within eighteen months and often end up in debt (the windfall effect). Legacy is more than money. It's clarity, intention, and stewardship. Families fracture over minor details when planning is unclear.

Review your estate plan regularly, especially after births, deaths, marriages, divorces, or major health changes or events. Work with trusted professionals. Update your documents. Fund your trust. Do the hard work now so your heirs don't face the much harder reality later.

KEY TAKEAWAYS

- Death is inevitable. Planning a successful legacy is not.
- After death, a person can no longer own or title assets.
- Planning requires choosing who receives, what they receive, how they receive it, and when.
- Planning is hard; however, not planning is even harder and can lead to confusion, chaos, and conflict.
- If you lack a written plan, the probate and intestate rules in your state will determine the outcome.
- A revocable living trust, or TOD or POD designations, can greatly reduce costs and stress.
- Write your plan and update it after major life events.
- A great legacy should leave your loved ones permanently and positively impacted.
- Great legacies are created by our *actions*. It is through these actions, not just ideas or good intentions, that outcomes and lasting impacts endure for our loved ones' lives.

Your IPAs (Not the Beer)

Write your *Identify Plan Actions* here:

IDENTIFIED item(s):

PLAN (your strategy):

ACTIONS (take a step forward):

7

A Financial Service Provider's Exposé: Behind the Curtain

We cannot unsee what we have already seen.

There is a stark contrast between planners and peddlers in the financial services industry. Based on my experience and observation, true planners likely represent only 10–20% of the profession. The difference is revealed quite simply: whether solutions begin with analysis and a process or with the sale of a product.

As a firm, we are drawn to solution-based advice and advisors, not salespeople. True advisors offer analysis for a fee, after which the client can choose their own providers and solutions. The fee is not wasted money if the value of a long-term relationship and the end results are the desired outcome. This approach does not work if "cheap" is the primary goal.

When I solicit bids for a particular project, I apply what I call the "rule of three" providers. I seldom choose the lowest bid, nor the highest. More often than not, the middle bid is the best overall value. On occasion, I am pleasantly surprised to receive a good price, service, and product—and to receive it quickly.

Rule: *Pick the two you desire most; all three are Nirvana.*

When I began my career in financial services around 1984, I was extensively trained in sales techniques, including the ABC (Always Be Closing) approach. Although this approach was widely accepted then, I instead gravitated toward a needs-based approach, focusing on identifying financial "gaps" and delivering solutions in a meaningful, purposeful way.

The planner mindset views the challenge—and themselves—as problem solvers offering solutions-based advice. The focus is on the desired outcome: revealing obstacles, removing obstructions, and then implementing the actions of the plan.

A Typical Story of Transparent Wealth Management

A new couple was introduced to us by a longtime client. They visited our website, reached out, and scheduled a consultation.

When they arrived for their first meeting, they came prepared. They brought thoughtful questions, along with organized copies of their investment statements, tax returns, insurance summaries, and estate planning documents. They had selected our Core 4 Solutions Analysis Program to determine what was on track—and what was not.

Our advisor began by asking intentional, specific questions. What were their dreams? Their goals? How did they truly feel about risk? What concerns kept them up at night? What outcomes did they most desire? With clarity around these answers, a follow-up results review meeting was scheduled.

Element One: Strategy and Execution

At their next meeting, we began with the first element of the Core 4 Solutions Analysis: Strategy and Execution. The risk analysis revealed how they felt about risk compared to how their investments were actually positioned. It showed what they could reasonably expect to gain when markets rise—and what they might lose when markets fall. In other words, it measured their risk-adjusted returns and alignment.

We then contrasted risk and return, taxes, and inflation with income, current spending, and projected future outlays. Under the stated assumptions, the planning software produced an illustrative probability-of-success score of 87 out of 99 for this hypothetical couple. Probability-of-success scores are tools used within financial planning software to help illustrate the sensitivity of a plan to different assumptions. They are not guarantees of any outcome, will change as inputs change, and should not be interpreted as a prediction of future results.

While encouraging, the findings also highlighted areas that needed adjustment to ensure they would not outlive their resources.

Element Two: Tax Efficiency

The second element focused on Tax Efficiency. Here, we discovered certain inefficiencies. Deductions available to them had not been fully utilized. We discussed options and provided a clear written summary for them to review with their tax professional, ensuring collaboration and alignment across their advisory team.

> *Any tax examples, strategies, deductions, or estate and beneficiary references in this book are general in nature and based on federal tax law and regulations in effect as of the date of writing. Tax laws are complex, are subject to change (including retroactively), and may differ at the state and local level. Nothing in this book is intended or written to be used, and cannot be used, for the purpose of avoiding U.S. federal, state, or local tax penalties or promoting, marketing, or recommending any transaction or matter to any person. Readers should consult their own qualified tax professional (CPA, Enrolled Agent, or tax attorney) and, where applicable, their estate-planning attorney regarding their specific circumstances before acting on any information contained in this book.*

Element Three: Protection and Insurance

The third element addressed Protection and Insurance. This analysis revealed where their coverage was strong, where it was lacking, and what was missing altogether. They were also shown the financial strength and independent ratings of their insurance carriers. A summary was prepared, and referrals were offered for second opinions on rates and coverage to ensure they were adequately covered.

Element Four: Legacy

Last—but certainly not least—was Legacy. Years earlier, they had completed a Revocable Living Trust. However, life had changed. When we compared their current wishes and desired outcomes to what their estate documents directed, the two no longer matched.

Our advisor began updating their estate plan through a qualified legal provider to bring everything back into alignment. We assured them this would not be a one-time review, but part of an ongoing process. Births, deaths, marriages, divorces, health events, and major life changes can all alter outcomes. Their plan would evolve as their lives evolve.

The Result

For this couple, now valued clients, our Transparent Wealth Management process was eye-opening. As it has been for many families over the past 43 years, gaps were identified, solutions were presented, and a clear plan and process were established to implement and monitor their progress. In this example, the score moved higher after adjustments; individual results for other clients or readers will differ and may be lower.

They expressed appreciation for the clarity of our process, the attention to detail, and the genuine concern shown for them and their heirs.

> *This testimonial was given by a current client of Rik Saylor Financial. No cash or non-cash compensation was paid or promised in exchange for this testimonial, and the client has no other material conflict of interest in providing it. The client's experience may not be representative of the experience of other clients. Past performance is not indicative of future results, and this testimonial is not a guarantee of any particular outcome. Please see Author Disclosures.*

As one longtime client once shared publicly:

"I place my faith in God and my financial confidence with Rik Saylor Financial."

We are deeply honored to serve our family of clients—their families, their friends, and their coworkers.

This is more than what we do.

It is our passion.

Our mission.

And our calling in life.

IDENTIFY – PLAN – ACTION

Ongoing: Measure, Monitor, and Adjust

Beginning with the sale of a product may completely miss the mark if it fails to consider the full scope of personal facts and circumstances. To me, this distinction reflects the difference between a transactional interaction and an ongoing relationship, as demonstrated through the planning process and approach. The salesperson's mindset often reflects an "eat what you kill" or "hit-and-run" scenario. This typically reveals itself through poor—or nonexistent—service and follow-up.

While self-interest is part of human nature, excessive self-interest can be identified by its negative impact on others. If a service provider does not see their self-interest or is unwilling to disclose it, they are either unaware or not being truthful. In either case, neither of these works for me personally.

Certain products and services provide trailing compensation to the service provider rather than a full upfront commission. Aligning yourself with someone through a trailing-pay structure can better align mutual interests—simply put, your advisor does better as you do.

It is an important question to ask whether someone is acting as a fiduciary or merely as a salesperson. Equally important is understanding the difference between fees and true total costs. While it matters what you pay for a product or service, it matters far more what the outcome may ultimately pay you.

Fees are what a provider charges directly. Total costs, however, can include taxes, custodial fees, transactional expenses, administrative fees, recurring charges, and even lost opportunity costs. Total cost may also include time commitments or backend charges required to exit a product (CDSC- Contingent Deferred Sales Charges). Planners typically have access to tools that measure these factors through professional subscriptions, though some resources are also available to laypersons.

When evaluating these relationships, I think in terms of three outcomes: win/win, lose/win, or win/lose. The most desirable—and sustainable—scenario is the win/win, where both the individual and the provider benefit. If one party wins while the other loses, the relationship is fundamentally flawed unless the arrangement is purely transactional.

I am not suggesting that paying a commission does not work. Rather, it is critical to know what you are trying to achieve and to operate from a full-disclosure mindset. Transparency tends to lead to accountability. In some cases, paying a commission can be cost-effective and still serve as an appropriate component of an overall plan.

Compensation is a universal element across nearly all industries. That said, fees tend to be higher with specialists than with a department-store-style approach offering a broad array of services. In such models, profit margins are spread across multiple offerings. The essential question to ask is whether you are paying only for what you actually need.

Personally, if I were diagnosed with cancer—God forbid—I would seek out the most qualified specialist for that specific condition rather than a general practitioner. I would also want to know their reviews and where they ranked in those reviews. After all, whether someone finished first or last in medical school, they are still called "doctor."

SEC, Broker-Dealers, and Registered Investment Advisors

The Securities and Exchange Commission (SEC) is the government regulatory agency responsible for overseeing securities transactions involving broker-dealers and Registered Investment Advisors (RIAs). (Securities Exchange Act of 1934)

Broker-dealers are regulated by FINRA, a self-regulatory organization operating under the SEC. Broker-dealers and their agents must adhere to the "Know Your Customer" rule. By contrast, RIAs generally operate under a fiduciary standard under applicable law, meaning they cannot transact in a manner that would harm the client unless the transaction is unsolicited.

Under Know Your Customer and suitability requirements, an adviser may recommend a product that aligns with a client's financial profile and objectives, even if other reasonably available alternatives could be more favorable to the client. This distinction is significant.

Through research—specifically a firm's ADV Part 2 brochure—clients can learn about the firm's Investment Policy Statement (IPS) provisions and overall approach.

Insurance Agents and Products

The insurance landscape includes a wide array of products serving different purposes. Property and casualty insurance (P&C) is necessary and effective in mitigating risk (see chapter 5 on protection). Health insurance is essential, as few individuals can afford the financial impact of a major illness without it.

In my experience, other products—such as certain annuities and life insurance policies—are often packaged and sold as tax havens or risk-free panaceas. Too often, these products over-promise and under-deliver.

Chapter Summary

This chapter pulls back the curtain on the financial services industry, distinguishing true planners from product-driven salespeople. We explored compensation structures, fiduciary responsibility, total cost awareness, and regulatory oversight, while emphasizing the value of transparency, alignment of interests, and long-term relationships over transactional thinking.

KEY TAKEAWAYS

- True planners focus on process and outcomes, not just products.
- Only a small percentage of the industry operates as genuine planners.
- Long-term advisory relationships often deliver more value than "cheap" solutions.
- Stop guessing and start measuring.
- The Rule of Three: Fast/Price/Quality helps identify optimal value; all three are Nirvana.
- Transactional sales models often result in poor service and follow-up.
- Trailing compensation can better align the interests of advisors and clients.
- Fees matter, but total costs and outcomes matter more.
- Win/win relationships are the only sustainable advisory model.
- Understanding the difference between fiduciary and sales standards is critical.
- Not all insurance or investment products deliver on their promises.

Your IPAs (Not the Beer)

Write your *Identify Plan Actions* here:

IDENTIFIED item(s):

PLAN (your strategy):

ACTIONS (take a step forward):

8

For Business Owners Only

Every business owner will inevitably exit, by succession or sale, potentially with a chest full of money because they planned... or on a gurney.

In addition to personal and financial considerations, there's your business. Akin to the three-legged stool, you need to address all three areas to be balanced. If one leg is weak or missing, everything becomes unstable. Most owners focus on the business and ignore personal planning. Yet 73% of owners regret selling their company, not because of price but because they sold their purpose. I frame this through the "Ys" of life: the year you were born, the year you discover why you are here, and what you do in between the "dashes."

It's a sad reality that 4 out of 5 businesses will not be transferred or survive to the next generation, mainly due to a lack of planning or preparation. Business owners are among the hardest-working people I know. They spend so much time working in the business that they rarely have time to work on it. The result is tragic. Someone's life's work simply disappears. In financial services, the failure rate is even higher: 9 out of 10.

The issue isn't intent. People don't plan to fail. They fail to plan. Lifestyle businesses and enterprise businesses operate very differently. In a lifestyle business, the owner is the business. When the owner leaves or dies, the business often dies too. Enterprise businesses, on the other hand, build equity, recurring revenue, and value multiples. That distinction shapes the future of the owners and their families.

I enjoy working with all types of owners, but I am especially drawn to those who are good and want to be great. I work with Main Street and midmarket businesses because small businesses have been part of my life from the start. I began my work at 13 with a paper route, had a construction business at age 20, and eventually moved into financial services at 23. Over 42 years in the financial industry and

28 years as the owner of my own firm have shown me how deeply rewarding this work can be, especially when helping owners solve challenges to grow, maintain, and exit with confidence. I obtained a CEPA (Certified Exit Planning Advisor) designation in 2020 and executed my own succession plan for Rik Saylor Financial, Inc.

An Owner's Story

Through my training as a CEPA, I learned that it typically takes 3-5 years to transform a well-run company into one that is built to sell. Of course, I always like a challenge, and I thought I could do it in half the time. SURPRISE! Even being equipped with the knowledge and tools, you guessed it, it took 3 years to complete my plan.

I had the same hurdles to overcome that many business owners do... devoting time to working on my business rather than day-to-day operations. Successful business owners know their business and are smart. However, the knowledge and skill set, as well as the team, required to systematize and execute a plan, are essential. ***Remember, you only get 1 chance to get this right!***

The Five Stages of Business Maturity

There are five stages of business maturity: **Identify, Protect, Build, Harvest,** and **Manage**. Each stage focuses on increasing business value and reducing risk.

> **Download "The 5 Stages of Business Maturity" and all the resources from this book at:** ***WealthWaveTools.com***

1. **Identify** what type of business category you're in and your "high multiple" competitors. The key metrics for any business are universal and unique and must be measured and improved to achieve the top valuation.
2. **Protect** what you have built by identifying the risks that are evident (5 Ds: Death, Divorce, Disability, Disagreement, and Disaster) and taking steps to secure them through legal and strategic systemization.
3. **Build:** High multiple companies do not happen by accident. It is intentional, methodical, and measurable.
4. **Harvest:** Reap the fruits of your lifetime of labor, what you have built, and *live your ideal life.* You can realize this at the same time you are growing enterprise value.
5. **Manage** your ongoing business by leading and systemizing the accountability in your "recipe" to assure the ongoing quality and continuity of your life's work.

The Four Intangible Growth Drivers

Four intangible capitals drive growth: **Human, Social, Customer, and Structural.**

Download "The 4 Intangibles" and all the resources from this book at*: WealthWaveTools.com*

1. **Human capital** is about the right people in the right seats and having a team of individuals who want it, get it, and possess the capacity to achieve it. They are loyal, intelligent, and quick/urgent in their executions—the proverbial "A" team.

2. **Social capital** is culture. Culture is everything; a team that fits together thrives together.
3. **Customer capital** focuses on revenue concentration and stability. Imagine having your ideal client profile and every one of them matching it. Repeat customers and clients refer new business just like themselves.
4. **Structural capital** comprises systems, processes, technology, and the knowledge that enable the business to run without the owner. Any company that doesn't have this is merely "winging it" and isn't as valuable or transferable.

Mind the Gap

Every business has gaps: **Profit, Wealth,** and **Value**. Most owners believe their businesses are better than they truly are. When you look closely, the opportunities become clear.

➔ **The Profit Gap:** The difference between what your company is earning/producing and what the maximum potential is.

➔ **The Wealth Gap:** The difference between where you are now and where your *ideal life* goals/dreams are.

➔ **The Value Gap:** The profit gap vs the potential sale price compared to the top multiple for comparable companies. It pays in spades to be "your ideal self."

Download "Know Your Gaps" and all the resources from this book at: *WealthWaveTools.com*

Build with the End in Mind

Owners walk two parallel paths: business and personal. These paths shape meaning and identity. Financial success without purpose can feel empty, and too many owners exit with no vision for the next 20 to 30 years of their lives, minus work. Without purpose, quality of life declines. There is also a unique paradox with vacations. When owners step away, things often go awry. This reveals a lack of systemization, processes, protocols, and continuity planning. A core reason many businesses fail to scale or transition is that running a good business is not necessarily the same as running one that is ready to exit. "*Built to sell*" is a great axiom to follow.

Experience taught me this the hard way. I learned to track KPIs (Key Performance Indicators) and SOPs (Standard Operating Procedures), and to prioritize the four areas that set good companies apart from great ones: *profitability, operations, sales, and continuity planning.* My advice: Stop guessing and start measuring. Every owner must prepare for the unexpected: death, divorce, disability, disagreement, or disaster. Everyone exits eventually. You can exit through intention or through default. One path can potentially deliver a chest full of money and peace of mind; the other is less likely to.

Owners must also prepare for crisis moments. When disaster strikes, a pandemic hits, or a recession rolls in, who do you call? How do you keep the business alive? These questions define exit readiness. The right team of professionals makes all the difference. This proactive approach is equally important when thinking about long-term goals and business evolution.

The solution statement is focused: *Begin with the end in mind.* Work backward to determine what must be done, when, and by whom. The right time to prepare is always earlier than expected. Growth can accelerate with the right coaching. I improved my sports endeavors by learning from someone farther along the path than I was. The same principle applies to business. A coach can bring clarity, accountability, and a path forward, and when relentless execution is in place, better results.

My calling grew from my upbringing. My parents taught me hard work, faith, and service. Financial planning became more than a career. It became a mission, especially once I saw how it changed lives. I realized my purpose aligned with helping others maximize their God-given talents. Money is simply a means for that purpose.

Business owners and the middle class are the backbone of America, yet they rarely have time to work on their businesses after a long week spent in them. Helping owners analyze, simplify, and apply proven strategies is meaningful and fulfilling work. This is why I love what I do. People often ask when I'll retire. The answer is simple. I'll continue the work as long as I make an impact, or until something more purposeful comes along.

Where is your plan at?

KEY TAKEAWAYS

- Most owners work *in* the business rather than *on* it, leaving them unprepared for the one exit everyone will eventually make, by design or by default.
- The strongest businesses intentionally move through the five stages of maturity and invest in the four intangible capitals that create real, transferable value.
- Every business has profit, wealth, and value gaps, and owners consistently overestimate their company's readiness; measuring, not guessing, reveals the truth.
- Built-to-sell companies are systemized, team-driven, and able to run without the owner; lifestyle businesses vanish when the owner does, or are sold at asset or fire-sale prices.
- Begin with the end in mind, build purpose alongside profit, and surround yourself with the right professionals because exiting well is never an accident; it's intentional.

Your IPAs (Not the Beer)

Write your *Identify Plan Actions* here:

IDENTIFIED item(s):

PLAN (your strategy):

ACTIONS (take a step forward):

Epilogue

"You never know who's swimming naked until the tide goes out."

—Warren Buffett

The Tide Always Returns

The market will continue to rise.

And it will continue to fall.

New headlines will replace old fears.

New bubbles will form where old ones burst.

Every boom and bust cycle has a beginning — a sharp ascent followed by an equally stark collapse, often returning to where it started… or lower.

Identify the trend.

Catch the wave.

Leave the party early when the momentum begins to fade.

But the tide is not your enemy.

It is your teacher.

In life, there are three resources entrusted to our stewardship: our time, our talents, and our treasure.

How we manage them profoundly impacts our lives, our loved ones, our communities, and our country as a whole.

The Parable of the Bags of Gold (Talents)

(From the New International Version (NIV), Gospel of Matthew 25:14–30)

Again, it will be like a man going on a journey, who called his servants and entrusted his wealth to them.

To one he gave five bags of gold, to another two bags, and to another one bag, each according to his ability. Then he went on his journey.

The man who had received five bags of gold went at once and put his money to work and gained five bags more.

So also, the one with two bags of gold gained two more.

But the man who had received one bag went off, dug a hole in the ground and hid his master's money.

After a long time the master of those servants returned and settled accounts with them.

The man who had received five bags of gold brought the other five.

"Master," he said, "you entrusted me with five bags of gold. See, I have gained five more."

His master replied, "Well done, good and faithful servant! You have been faithful with a few things; I will put you in charge of many things. Come and share your master's happiness!"

The man with two bags of gold also came.

"Master," he said, "you entrusted me with two bags of gold; see, I have gained two more."

His master replied, "Well done, good and faithful servant! You have been faithful with a few things; I will put you in charge of many things. Come and share your master's happiness!"

Then the man who had received one bag of gold came.

"Master," he said, "I knew that you are a hard man, harvesting where you have not sown and gathering where you have not scattered seed. So I was afraid and went out and hid your gold in the ground. See, here is what belongs to you."

His master replied, "You wicked, lazy servant! So you knew that I harvest where I have not sown and gather where I have not scattered seed? Well then, you should have put my money on deposit with the bankers, so that when I returned I would have received it back with interest. So take the bag of gold from him and give it to the one who has ten bags. For whoever has will be given more, and they will have an abundance. Whoever does not have, even what they have will be taken from them."

Throughout this book, we have explored the difference between motion and progress, between noise and signal, between planners and peddlers.

The waves will test you. They always do.

The question is not whether volatility will come —

It is whether you will be anchored when it does.

True wealth is not built in moments of excitement.

It is built in seasons of discipline.

When the tide goes out, it reveals what was built on rock —

and what was built on sand.

Your financial life is not a scoreboard.

It is a stewardship assignment.

If you navigate with patience, integrity, and clarity of purpose,

The waves that once frightened you will become the very force that carries you forward.

The ocean does not apologize for its movement.

It simply moves.

So should you.

A Call to Action

Some investors love the market and the challenges it presents. For them, it is a game — an attempt to "beat the street" and master its rhythms.

Are you a DIY investor, or are you seeking true professional guidance?

Financial markets operate approximately 6.5 hours per trading day, totaling roughly 252 trading days per year. Effective portfolio management requires a structured and disciplined approach within this framework.

Our firm's guiding values — Genuine. Intentional. Personable. Passionate. — are evident in everything we do.

If you are a moderately hands-on to hands-off investor with $750,000 or more, reach out for a second opinion on your current strategy and plan. We invite you to explore our approach and services at:

www.riksaylorfinancial.com

Continuity and continual care for our family of clients are values we all share.

If you are an advisor with a book of $50 million or more and desire to be part of a growing, client-first family, we should talk…

rik@riksaylorfinancial.com

Wealth is the means — not the end.

The end is to live our ideal life by changing lives for the better.

Regardless of your personal beliefs, all principled people desire to finish strong.

And at the very end, to hear the sweetest of words:

"Welcome home, my good and faithful servant."

Rik Saylor
March 31, 2026

Acknowledgments

I now understand why it has taken me 30 years to write this book... because writing is hard work. The book you're holding in your hands, reading electronically, or listening to on audio, is the culmination of conversations, lessons, and experiences spanning my entire 43 years in the financial services industry.

As with most meaningful accomplishments, the right people appeared at the right moments to help bring this work together. I'd like to thank my publishing team at Remarkable Press. Mark Imperial carries the same passion for publishing as I do for the world of wealth management, and his guidance and encouragement were instrumental in bringing this book to life.

I'm equally grateful for my team at Rik Saylor Financial, whose dedication and support made this project possible. Their contributions in technology, creativity, and collaboration were invaluable. While I may be the visionary, Robin Raper is the resourceful implementer who wears many hats and contributes in countless ways—from coordinating the details to creating innovative solutions that move ideas forward.

Everyone on our team has made a tremendous impact on the people we serve. My sincere thanks to Eric Hamberg, Nate Parker, and Amber Reckner for their commitment, professionalism, and shared mission.

I would also like to recognize the many colleagues throughout the financial services industry whom I have had the privilege to engage with over the decades. Through conversations, collaborations, and shared insights, you have contributed to the ideas and perspectives reflected in these pages.

Finally, I extend my deepest appreciation to our family of clients—both past and present. Thank you for the trust, confidence, and faith you place in us each day to help guide you toward your ideal lives. We do not take that responsibility lightly. It is an honor to serve you and your families with passion, professionalism, and care in the intentional and genuine manner that you expect and deserve.

- Rik Saylor

About Rik Saylor, IAR, CEPA

"Rik" James Henrik Saylor, IAR, CEPA, is a lifelong third-generation resident of Southwestern Ohio. The sole living and second son of four boys, born to Jim and Rose Ann (Dunkle) Saylor, Rik was raised with love, faith, a strong work ethic, an entrepreneurial spirit, a solid foundation—and given "wings to fly."

He and his wife, Kim, his soulmate of 25 years, share a blended family of five grown children and are loving, passionate Papaw and Mimi to four grandchildren. They lead very active lives, playing pickleball and golf, and hosting concerts at their lake house each summer. Kim jokingly says that grandchildren are a "mother's reward for not eating her young."

This is Rik's first full-length book and his second overall. He was one of ten contributing authors to Exit Smart, published in 2023, written for business owners who desire to grow, maintain, and sell their companies.

He is the Founder, President & CEO of Rik Saylor Financial Inc., established in 1997, and began his career in the financial services industry in 1984. In 2021, after completing his own succession plan, he transitioned to Managing Partner alongside Eric Hamberg, CFP®, Vice President, and his trusted right-hand advisor of 19 years.

In April 2023, he founded REDDE-ZONE Business Consulting LLC to guide and coach business owners in achieving their IDEAL LIVES. He engages owners from a personal, business, and financial perspective, helping Main Street to middle market companies improve, specializing in businesses that are good and aspire to become great. Ultimately, he helps transition "built to sell" enterprises to the next generation of entrepreneurs who desire to continue their legacies successfully.

What People Who Know Us Are Saying...

"Working with Rik Saylor Financial has been a very positive experience. The team consistently takes the time to understand my goals, both personal and for my business. As a younger business owner who isn't planning to exit anytime soon, I appreciate how their approach is truly tailored to my situation, adapting strategies that fit my timeline and risk comfort.

I also value the holistic nature of their service. Beyond investment planning, they've provided thoughtful referrals and resources that have been genuinely useful to me, like connecting me with a CPA and accounting, advising on 401(k) plan options for my company, and even helping guide large asset purchases. Communication is excellent and responsive, which gives me peace of mind that my questions and evolving needs are being heard and addressed thoughtfully.

I'm glad to have continued working with them after my father's experience with the firm, and I feel that their guidance and support have helped me manage the complexities of both personal and business financial decisions with greater clarity and confidence."

- Adam S.
  Business owner & client since 2013

"Working with Rik Saylor Financial has always felt personal and genuine. They've taken the time to really get to know me, not just my finances, and that has made all the difference.

I've always felt heard, respected, and supported, even when I didn't fully understand everything. They've helped me feel more organized and confident about my decisions. I truly appreciate the care and interest they show in me and my family."

- Marilyn S.
  Client since 2017

"I've had a pleasant and honest relationship with Rik Saylor Financial for over a decade. When my wife and I first started thinking seriously about our future and retirement, we knew we wanted professional guidance. Over the years, they've given us the knowledge and confidence to feel much more organized about our financial planning.

I've especially appreciated how personalized their advice has been. For example, Nate Parker once took the time to review the fine print on an annuity I was considering. He suggested waiting just six months before drawing from it, which ended up making a real difference for us. That kind of careful attention stands out.

The team is always responsive—just a quick call or email away—and they genuinely listen to understand what matters to us. I feel they've guided us with a thoughtful, conservative approach that fits our needs and values.

I've been comfortable enough with them to refer many friends and family over the years, which speaks to the trust I have in them. For anyone wanting honest, personalized financial guidance, I'd gladly share my experience with Rik Saylor Financial."

- C. Hatcher
  Client since 2013

Please see Author Disclosures

"Working with Rik Saylor Financial has been an excellent experience for me and my family. They've always treated us with professionalism and respect while taking the time to explain things in a way that's easy to understand.

I've felt truly heard and supported, knowing their advice is tailored to my needs and grounded in knowing me and my family personally. Their communication is always clear and responsive, and I've been able to approach my goals with greater confidence and organization.

It means a lot to work with a team that has been there for my parents for years and continues to provide thoughtful guidance for all of us."

- Michael B.
  Family clients since 2007

These testimonials were given by current clients of Rik Saylor Financial. No cash or non-cash compensation was paid or promised in exchange for this testimonial, and the clients have no other material conflict of interest in providing it. The client's experience may not be representative of the experience of other clients. Past performance is not indicative of future results, and this testimonial is not a guarantee of any particular outcome.

Advisory Services offered through Rik Saylor Financial, a registered investment adviser.

This book is provided for informational and educational purposes only and is not intended as investment, tax, legal, accounting, or other professional advice. The content is general in nature and may not apply to your specific circumstances. Nothing in this book constitutes a recommendation, offer, or solicitation to buy or sell any security or to engage in any investment strategy. Reading this book does not create an advisory relationship or a fiduciary relationship with the author, publisher, or any affiliated entity.

Investing involves risk, including the possible loss of principal. Any past performance mentioned is not indicative of future results. Any references to market returns, indices, asset classes, securities, strategies, or financial products are for illustration only and may not be suitable for all investors. Indexes are unmanaged and cannot be invested in directly. Any projections, forecasts, charts, hypothetical illustrations, model results, or examples are provided for educational purposes only, are based on assumptions that may not occur, and may not reflect the impact of fees, expenses, trading costs, taxes, inflation, or the timing of contributions and withdrawals, all of which can materially affect results. Outcomes will vary with market conditions and individual circumstances.

Tax laws and regulations are complex and subject to change. Any discussion of tax-related concepts is general in nature and may not reflect current law or your situation. You should consult your own tax, legal, and financial professionals regarding your specific circumstances before acting on any information in this book. Reliance on any information in this book is solely at your own risk.

Testimonials, endorsements, and client experiences reflect the views and experiences of the individuals quoted as of the date provided and may not be representative of the experience of all clients or readers. No cash compensation was provided for any testimonial or endorsement. If any individual received a non-cash benefit in connection with providing a testimonial or endorsement, for example, a free copy of the book or public recognition, that benefit will be disclosed where applicable in that section. Testimonials and endorsements are not a guarantee of future performance or success, and individual results will vary.

The author and publisher make no representations or warranties regarding the accuracy, completeness, or timeliness of the information in this book. To the fullest extent permitted by law, the author, publisher, and any affiliated parties disclaim any liability for any direct or indirect loss or damage arising from actions taken or not taken based on the content of this book.